Point-and-Click!
A Guide to SPSS for Windows

Fifth Edition

Larry A. Pace, Ph.D.

TwoPaces.com

Anderson, SC

Larry A. Pace

Point-and-Click! A Guide to SPSS® for Windows®, 5th Edition

ISBN 978-0-9799775-7-2

Published in the United States of America by

TwoPaces.com
102 San Mateo Dr.
Anderson, SC 29625

Preface and Acknowledgements

This point-and-click guide provides basic information for students and instructors in statistics and research methods classes who want to learn how to use SPSS® for Windows®. This book shows screens from IBM SPSS Statistics 20 running in Windows 7. If you are using a different version of SPSS or of Windows, or a Mac rather than a PC, your screens may look different from the screen shots shown.

In my personal library, there are dozens of books on how to do statistics, including five books on using SPSS within arm's reach. You may wonder why anyone would need to write another book about SPSS. The answer is really quite simple. Most books on SPSS are either too technical for the average student, or so easy (and so watered down) that the student learns nothing at all (except how to point and click to make SPSS produce output). I wrote this book as an instruction manual. If you follow along, reproduce the screens you see in this book, and read the accompanying explanations of what the screens are telling you, you will learn how to use SPSS, and you will learn (or relearn) quite a bit about statistics at the same time.

In addition to presenting the most common statistical procedures, this book shows you how to establish an effective data structure, examine data distributions, and conduct exploratory data analyses. You will learn how to test distributional assumptions and how to select and perform appropriate nonparametric alternatives when your data violate these parametric assumptions. A new chapter on bootstrapping (Chapter 15) illustrates how modern robust statistics can be used as an effective alternative to traditional null hypothesis significance testing.

This book is useful not just for a statistics or research design class, but also for future reference when you need a quick refresher for a particular analysis in SPSS. By following the examples in this book, you will learn how the program works, and you will soon be able to figure out how to perform other procedures by examining the SPSS menus, options, and dialogs.

The data sets used in this book, along with many additional resources, are available at a companion web page located at the following URL:

http://twopaces.com/SPSSBook.html

This book is intended for the absolute beginner, someone who has never used SPSS 20 and who needs to learn quickly and independently how to use the program. SPSS has a rich and powerful option for manual programming (SPSS syntax), which we will touch on briefly in Chapter 15. This text is not a complete SPSS reference, of which there are many, including the SPSS help files, tutorials, and case studies themselves. This book is also not a statistics text, though it delves into statistical theory and assumptions on several occasions. Instead, this book covers the procedures the reader is most likely to encounter in a basic research design and statistics class in psychology or another behavioral science.

The reader should start with the basics in Chapter 1, and then go on to working with data in Chapter 2. Descriptive statistics are the subject of Chapter 3, and Chapter 4 introduces exploratory data analysis and testing normality of distribution. From that point forward, every chapter is a standalone tutorial. You can consider Chapters 14 and 15 optional, but I encourage you at least to glance at them in case you decide later that you need to do data restructuring (Chapter 14) or bootstrapping (Chapter 15). Though many chapters use common data sets, each chapter is self-contained so that you can learn or teach the material in any order you like—as well as skip the sections or chapters that are not relevant for you.

Because SPSS has become easier to use and increasingly more capable over the years, students and researchers can perform very complex analyses without knowing how to interpret the output or even knowing whether they chose the appropriate procedure. This problem is compounded by the fact that there are often several different ways to accomplish the same purpose, some easier to do, some harder, and many equivalent to one another, so that the choice is merely one of personal preference.

For all the reasons discussed above, this book provides a clear example of the kinds of research questions a particular technique addresses, and then shows the reader a direct way to accomplish that statistical goal using SPSS's point-and-click graphical interface.

No book, even one with a single author, is ever the work of a single person. This book started out as a series of tutorials that I wrote for Furman University. Those tutorials (still available and still useful, according to many e-mail testimonials) were based on SPSS version 15. The original idea of posting SPSS tutorials on the web for students to learn SPSS independently came from my friend and colleague Dr. Gil Einstein at Furman. I am also very grateful to Dr. Allen Huffcutt of Bradley University for his continued support for this project and for his careful review of the previous version. My good friend Dr. Kate Andrews, now of the University of the Rockies, was kind enough to serve as an external reviewer as well. My friend and colleague Dr. Lê Xuân Hy of Seattle University has served not only as a reviewer, but also has classroom-tested previous versions of this book, as well as several of my other books.

I would like to acknowledge my wife Shirley Pace, who has shown me the true meaning of love and loyalty.

About the Author

Larry A. Pace, Ph.D. is a Graduate Research Professor at Keiser University. He teaches courses in mathematical, psychological, and business statistics at the undergraduate and graduate levels. He was a Professor in the College of Undergraduate Studies at Argosy University from 2008 to 2012. Previously, he was Professor of Psychology and Chair of the Behavioral Sciences Department at Anderson University in Anderson, SC. Prior to joining Anderson University, he was an instructional development consultant for social sciences for Furman University in Greenville, SC. Larry is an award-winning professor of behavioral and business statistics, psychology, and management. His research interests include statistics education, data entry procedures, and collaborative learning, along with an ongoing research program to study students' and faculty members' attitudes toward plagiarism and other forms of academic dishonesty. He has published 20 books and more than 100 chapters, articles, and reviews. Additionally, he has written hundreds of online articles, reviews, and tutorials.

After earning a Ph.D. in psychological measurement from the University of Georgia, Larry taught at Rensselaer Polytechnic Institute before moving to Xerox Corporation to work as a personnel consultant and organization effectiveness manager. After nine years with Xerox, he returned to academe to teach at the University of Tennessee, and has since worked full-time at LSU-Shreveport, Louisiana Tech University, Clemson University, Furman University, Anderson University, Argosy University, and Keiser University. He has taught undergraduate and graduate courses in behavioral and business statistics, research methods, management, mathematics, sociology, education, and human resource development for Keiser University, Western Carolina University, Tri-County Technical College, Clemson University, Ashford University, University of the Rockies, Capella University, and Austin Peay State University. Over the years, he has served as a trainer, facilitator, internal and external consultant, psychology and management professor, MBA program director, business school dean, master's degree program coordinator, instructional development consultant, and academic department chair.

Larry lives in Anderson, South Carolina, with his wife Shirley Pace. The Paces have four grown children and two grandsons. They volunteer with Meals on Wheels and Keep America Beautiful. The Paces are also pet lovers with (currently) five cats and one dog, all rescued.

Larry has many hobbies and interests including music (he plays several instruments), reading, writing about statistics and research, writing poetry, woodcarving, cooking on the grill, hosting gatherings of friends and family, and tending a small vegetable garden and giving away fresh and pickled jalapeños, homemade salsa, tomatoes, beans, and corn. In a long-ago world before there were pocket calculators, cell phones, and personal computers, Larry carried a slide rule and programmed in FORTRAN-IV on a mainframe computer. He also played in a famously local rock band complete with groupies while attending high school and college.

Brief Contents

Table of Contents

1 SPSS Files and Windows

Objectives

1. Launch SPSS.
2. Examine different SPSS windows.
3. Learn about SPSS file types.

Overview

At the outset, a brief note is in order concerning the name of the software program illustrated in this book. IBM purchased SPSS, Inc. in 2009. As part of its focus on the use of the software for predictive analytics, IBM changed the program's name from SPSS to PASW (predictive analytics software) when version 17.0.3 was released. The name PASW persisted in version 18. With version 19, IBM returned to the much more familiar name SPSS. For the sake of simplicity, the name SPSS will be used throughout this book, even though your program may display the name PASW Statistics.

In a typical SPSS session, you will work with two or more SPSS windows and may save the results of your work for future use. In this introductory lesson, you will launch SPSS, examine various SPSS windows, and learn about the different kinds of SPSS files.

This book uses a shorthand way to refer to the menu-driven point-and-click interface of SPSS. When you should click on the "Descriptives" option under the "Descriptive Statistics" submenu under the "Analyze" menu, the instructions state more directly that you should select **Analyze > Descriptive Statistics > Descriptives**. Buttons and menu items or links you should click on appear in **boldface**, such as **OK**. Variable names are in *italics*. For example, when referring to a named variable such as Sex, the book refers to that variable as *Sex*. When you must type information into an SPSS window, that information is shown in `Courier New` font, as follows:

```
Quiz1 + Quiz2
```

The most effective way to learn from this book is to launch SPSS and to follow along with the step-by-step instructions. If you can reproduce the screens shown in this book by following the instructions, you will learn a great deal about how to use SPSS for basic statistics. You will also learn how the SPSS point-and-click interface works. This will enable you to explore additional procedures and options as your knowledge and confidence increase.

Changes to SPSS with Newer Versions

This book is a complete revision of *Point-and-Click! Guide to SPSS for Windows, Fourth Edition* (Pace, 2008), which illustrated SPSS 17.0 for Windows. The version of SPSS illustrated in this book is IBM SPSS Statistics 20 (with a few screens from version 19). The user of previous versions of SPSS will notice immediate differences in the newest versions of SPSS. IBM continues to change the appearance of the user interface. The functionality of the program has also been improved, and there are now many options and customization features unavailable in earlier versions. The unfortunate outcome is that SPSS is now even harder to learn than it was previously because there are often several (sometimes many) ways to accomplish the same purpose.

Launching SPSS

After installing SPSS, you must launch the program. To launch SPSS, double-click on the SPSS Statistics 20 icon. Depending on the way your computer is set up, you may find the icon on your desktop, in your Start Menu, or under **Start** > **All Programs** > **IBM SPSS Statistics** > **IBM SPSS Statistics 20** (see Figure 1-1). If you use the program frequently, you will find it convenient to copy the SPSS icon to your Windows desktop as a shortcut.

Figure 1-1. SPSS Statistics 20 icon

After locating the SPSS icon, click on it to launch SPSS. By default, you will see the SPSS opening dialog (splash screen) shown in Figure 1-2. This opening screen gives you various options including typing in data, running queries, opening data files, accessing database files to run new queries, and running the SPSS tutorial. If you prefer not to see this opening screen at program launch, you can check the box in front of "Don't show this dialog in the future" (see Figure 1-2).

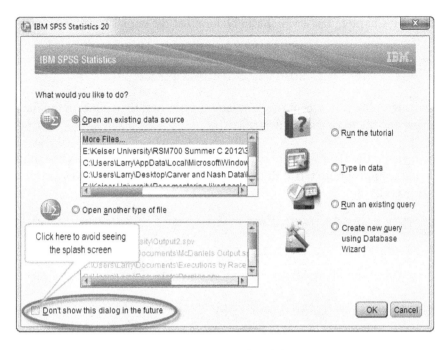

Figure 1-2. *SPSS opening window*

The SPSS Data Editor

If you click on **Cancel** or select "Type in data" and then click **OK**, the SPSS Data Editor will open with a blank data set, ready for you to begin typing or pasting data (see Figure 1-3).

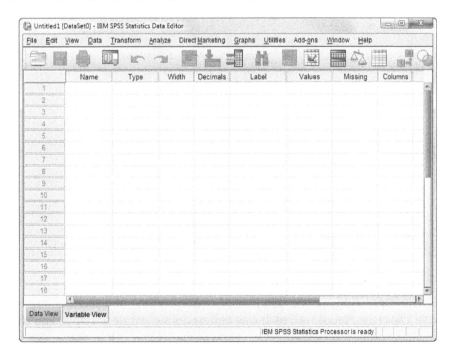

Figure 1-3. *SPSS Data Editor ready for creating a new data file*

If instead of selecting "Type in data," or "Cancel," you select "Open an existing data source," SPSS will allow you to navigate to any directory to retrieve an SPSS data file or some other data source. Let us open the data file associated with this chapter, Chapter_1.sav, which can be found at the book's companion web page at the following URL:

http://twopaces.com/SPSSBook.html

To retrieve the file, navigate to the data sets at the companion page, and then click on the file name to open it in SPSS or right-click to save the file to your hard drive.

The Data Editor has two views: the Data View shown in Figure 1-4 and the Variable View shown in Figure 1-5. To change the view, click on the appropriate tab at the bottom of the Data Editor window to select Data View or Variable View (see Figure 1-4).

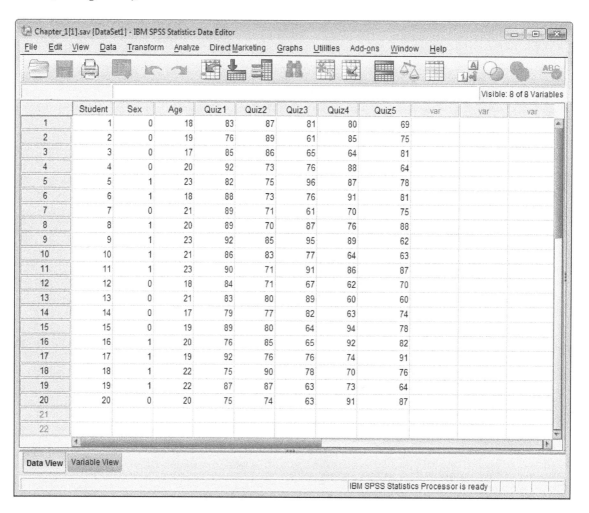

Figure 1-4. SPSS Data Editor view of an existing data file (Data View)

In the Data View, each row represents a single case (record or participant), and each column represents a separate variable. In the Variable View (see Figure 1-5), each row represents a separate variable. You can specify the structure of the data including the variable name, variable type, variable width in characters, number of decimals, a variable label, value labels, the manner of dealing with missing values, display column width, cell alignment, and the type of measure (nominal, ordinal or scale). We explore these settings in more detail in Chapter 2. When you save the contents of the SPSS Data Editor, you automatically save both the actual data values shown in the Data View and the data structure shown in the Variable View. To save the data file, click on **File** > **Save** and give the file a descriptive name. SPSS data files have the *.sav extension.

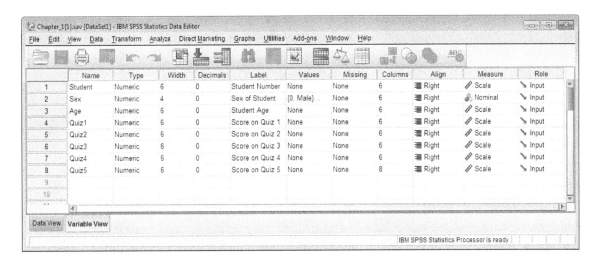

Figure 1-5. SPSS Data Editor view of an existing data file (Variable View)

The SPSS Viewer

In addition to the SPSS Data Editor, you will quickly become familiar with the SPSS Statistics Viewer (see Figure 1-6). This window shows the SPSS output. The SPSS Viewer opens whenever you run a procedure, and any new output appears at the end of the open viewer window. When you are finished with a particular analysis, you can save the contents of the SPSS Viewer in a separate file.

SPSS output files from versions 15.0 and lower had the *.spo extension. For SPSS versions 16.0 and higher, viewer files have the *.spv extension. When you save the output, it is okay to use the same name for a viewer file that you use with the related data file because the extensions are different. For example, you could open this chapter's data file, Chapter_1.sav, and save the associated viewer file with the name Chapter_1.spv. This would make the connection between the two files very clear.

Examine the SPSS Viewer window (Figure 1-6). Note the tree-like outline structure in the left pane, and the SPSS syntax in the right pane, in which the output also appears. You can choose to have SPSS display the syntax generated by the point-and-click commands, or you can turn off that feature. Although much of the SPSS output in this book shows syntax, we discuss only the point-and-click interface to access SPSS commands, features, and options in the first 14 chapters of this book. In Chapter 15, we briefly use syntax to generate samples from a normal distribution.

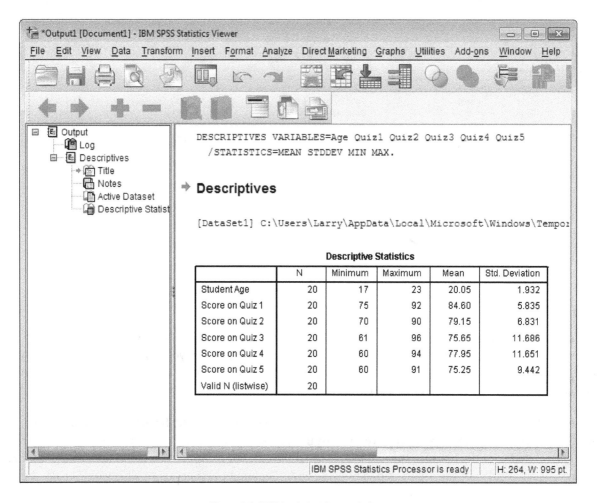

Figure 1-6. SPSS Statistics Viewer window

You can copy objects from the SPSS viewer and paste them into applications like Microsoft Word when you are writing your research reports. You can also send your output to a printer or export the output as an RTF file for word processing. From the outline view, you can select and print single or multiple output sections, collapse or expand the view, and rearrange and delete output sections.

SPSS Menus and Dialogs

Many SPSS dialogs require you to enter a variable or variables from a list in the left pane of the window into fields or panes on the right. To do so, use the small arrow button between the two panes. Select the variable or variables from the list by clicking on their names, and then click on the arrow button beside the field into which you want to move the variable. If you make a mistake, you can select the variable name and then press the arrow (which is now pointing back to the variable list) to return the variable to the list. If you make a big mistake, you can usually find a **Reset** button that allows you to begin the variable selection again (see Figure 1-7). The **Cancel** button will close the window, while the **Reset** button will clear the Variable list and move all the variables back to the left pane.

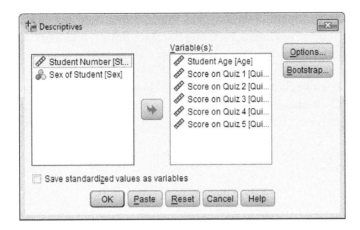

Figure 1-7. Cancel and Reset buttons

Recalling a Dialog

SPSS shows your selections in a dialog box, and you can recall and reuse these boxes. Recalling a dialog is often much faster than entering all the information again when you want to change an option or run an analysis again. Clicking on the **Recall Dialog** icon will bring up a list of the most recent dialogs (see Figure 1-8).

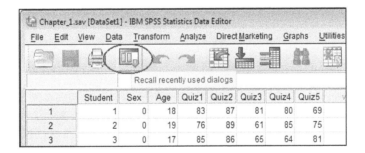

Figure 1-8. The Recall Dialog icon

Getting to the Goodies

Visit the companion web page for this book for all the data sets used in the text plus many additional resources. As a reminder, the web page is located at the following URL:

http://twopaces.com/SPSSBook.html

Further Reading

In addition to the basics covered in this book, SPSS is capable of sophisticated intermediate, advanced, and multivariate statistical analysis. After you have mastered the procedures in this introductory book, you may want to refer to the more complete references by Cronk (2008), Field (2005), George and Mallery (2009), Green and Salkind (2008), Norušis (2009), and Sweet and Grace-Martin (2008).

Chapter 1 Exercises

1. Launch SPSS 20 and examine the SPSS Data Editor's Data and Variable Views. Examine the SPSS Viewer, and note the outline view and the output window. Exit SPSS.

2. Launch SPSS, and from the opening screen, click the "radio button" in front of "Run the tutorial." Follow the step-by-step tutorials for reading data, using the Data Editor, and working with output. Examine the case studies and the statistics coach.

3. Exit SPSS. Launch SPSS and click on "Cancel." From the Data Editor, click on Help in the menu bar. Click on Statistics Coach. "Click on Summarize, describe, or present data." Note the Previous and Next buttons at the top right of the screen. Click on "Data in categories" and work through the statistics coach.

4. List and describe the major SPSS windows and file types.

2 Working with Data

Objectives

1. Establish an effective data structure.
2. Enter and delete records and variables.
3. Compute and save a new variable.

Overview

In this chapter, you will learn the basics of working with data and variables in SPSS. In addition to the option of typing data directly into SPSS using the Data Editor, one can open a variety of file types. Launch SPSS and select **File > Open > Data**. In the resulting dialog box, click on the arrow at the right of "Files of type:" and examine the various file types. You can open Excel files as well as text files and files from many other programs.

Assume you need to summarize the grades for 20 students on five separate quizzes. You want to determine the average score on each quiz and to calculate the average of the five quiz scores for each student. You also have information concerning each student's age in years and the student's sex, coded as 0 (*Male*) and 1 (*Female*). The data appear in Table 2-1 below. Although you can retrieve a copy of this data set, Chapter_2.sav, from the companion web page, it is also very beneficial to enter the data oneself for practice.

Table 2-1 Example data

Student	Sex	Age	Quiz1	Quiz2	Quiz3	Quiz4	Quiz5
1	0	18	83	87	81	80	69
2	0	19	76	89	61	85	75
3	0	17	85	86	65	64	81
4	0	20	92	73	76	88	64
5	1	23	82	75	96	87	78
6	1	18	88	73	76	91	81
7	0	21	89	71	61	70	75
8	1	20	89	70	87	76	88
9	1	23	92	85	95	89	62
10	1	21	86	83	77	64	63
11	1	23	90	71	91	86	87
12	0	18	84	71	67	62	70
13	0	21	83	80	89	60	60
14	0	17	79	77	82	63	74
15	0	19	89	80	64	94	78
16	1	20	76	85	65	92	82
17	1	19	92	76	76	74	91
18	1	22	75	90	78	70	76
19	1	22	87	87	63	73	64
20	0	20	75	74	63	91	87

Establishing an Effective Data Structure

Use the Variable View to establish your data structure. You can do this before or after entering the data records. Assume we plan to type the data directly into the Data Editor, as discussed above. To make the data entry easier and more productive, we will start with the Variable View and name our variables and define their structure before entering data. Look at the example data set (see Table 2.1). You see a student number, student sex, student age, and the five quiz scores. Although SPSS automatically numbers the rows of the data file, it is wise to provide a separate subject, case, or participant record number. This is helpful when you sort records in the SPSS file and then later want to return the data to their original state.

We will name and define the variables, adjust the column widths and decimals, and provide descriptive labels. We will also provide information concerning the scale of measurement. In many cases, the defaults provided by SPSS are adequate. But in many others they are not, and you should spend time in the Variable View understanding the various options. To establish a data structure either before or after entering data, follow these steps.

1. Open an SPSS data file. If you are entering new data, launch SPSS and create a blank data set as described in Chapter 1.
2. Click on the Variable View tab at the bottom of the SPSS Data Editor Window.
3. Enter the desired information for each variable in the data set.

As a rule of thumb, each row of the data file should represent only one record (participant, subject, or case). If you have multiple measures for that record, each measure should appear in a separate column (variable) within that row. For example, if you have a before and after measure for each participant, these two measures should be in separate columns in your data file.

If there are grouping variables, whether because of an experimental manipulation or as the result of a naturally occurring grouping such as sex or class standing, a column should be devoted to each such grouping variable. For example, if there are two independent groups, you should enter a column for group membership; the entries could be 0 and 1 or 1 and 2 to indicate the group to which a record belongs. We must suspend the one-row-per-participant rule in some situations. We deal with one such exception in Chapter 9.

Example Data Structure

Figure 2-1 illustrates a model SPSS data structure for the example data from Table 2-1. Access the Variable View by clicking on the tab at the bottom (see Figure 1-4). Enter the appropriate names for each variable as shown in Figure 2-1.

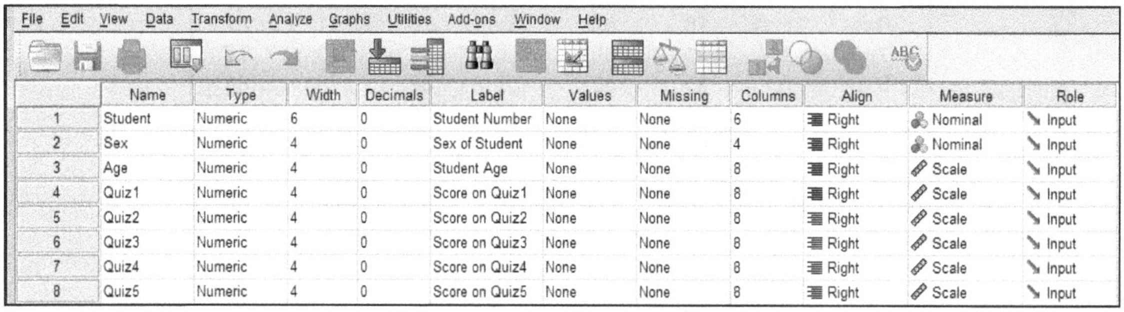

	Name	Type	Width	Decimals	Label	Values	Missing	Columns	Align	Measure	Role
1	Student	Numeric	6	0	Student Number	None	None	6	Right	Nominal	Input
2	Sex	Numeric	4	0	Sex of Student	None	None	4	Right	Nominal	Input
3	Age	Numeric	4	0	Student Age	None	None	8	Right	Scale	Input
4	Quiz1	Numeric	4	0	Score on Quiz1	None	None	8	Right	Scale	Input
5	Quiz2	Numeric	4	0	Score on Quiz2	None	None	8	Right	Scale	Input
6	Quiz3	Numeric	4	0	Score on Quiz3	None	None	8	Right	Scale	Input
7	Quiz4	Numeric	4	0	Score on Quiz4	None	None	8	Right	Scale	Input
8	Quiz5	Numeric	4	0	Score on Quiz5	None	None	8	Right	Scale	Input

***Figure 2-1.** Adding variable information*

Variable names should be short and should not contain spaces or special characters other than perhaps underscores. If you are working with an older version of SPSS, variable names may be limited to eight characters, and will display in lowercase letters only. Regardless of the SPSS version you are using, you can enter longer descriptive labels in the Labels field. These labels can include spaces. SPSS defaults to a numeric data type with 8 characters and 2 decimals. Examine Figure 2-1 and locate the column labeled "Measure." "Scale" measurement, represented by a ruler icon, is the default and includes interval and ratio measures. You can change this setting to nominal or ordinal by clicking in the variable worksheet. Let us change the decimal settings to zero, modify the column and display widths, and change the measurement type for *Student* number and *Sex* to nominal (see Figure 2-1). As the last steps in establishing the data structure, enter descriptive labels for each variable and enter variable labels for *Sex*, so that we will not be confused later as to whether we used 1 for males or for females. These modifications to the data structure appear in Figure 2-1. You may think this process of defining a data structure is tedious and unnecessary. But you will thank yourself later for taking the time to learn it, as it is valuable for labeling your research results, a nice thing to do for others who might use your data in the future, and a helpful memory jogger when you return to a data file after an extended absence.

To enter the value labels for *Sex*, open the Variable View and then click in the Values cell in the row for *Sex*. Locate a small button at the right end of the cell. Click on that button to access the Value Labels dialog shown in Figure 2-2. Here you can enter the values and their labels. Enter 0 as the value and Male as the label for that value, and then click on **Add** to enter the value and label. Next enter 1 as the value and Female as its label. SPSS puts quotes around the labels (see Figure 2-3). If there are more than two values, repeat this process until all the values have appropriate labels.

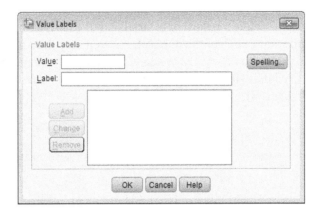

Figure 2-2. Value Labels dialog

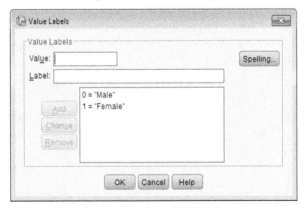

Figure 2-3. Completed value labels

Before or after establishing your data structure, you can type your data directly into SPSS from the Data Editor. As mentioned previously, best practice calls for establishing the data structure before entering or opening data files.

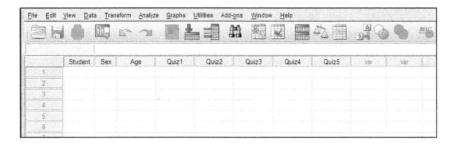

Figure 2-4. *Data View reveals a blank data set with variable names*

In addition to typing data directly into the Data Editor, SPSS also allows you to open existing SPSS data files, spreadsheet files such as Microsoft Excel workbooks, database files, and other kinds of data. It is also possible to paste data from tables and worksheets into the SPSS Data Editor.

Deleting a Record or Variable

There may be times when you need to delete a record or a variable. For example, you may see that you have entered the same record twice and want to delete the duplicate. Or you may determine that there is some problem with a record and find it easier to delete it and start over again. Similarly, you may have created a new variable and later decide that you do not need it anymore. Assume you accidentally entered the data twice for student number 20 in the data set (see Figure 2-5).

*Chapter_2.sav [DataSet1] - IBM SPSS Statistics Data Editor

File   Edit   View   Data   Transform   Analyze   Direct Marketing   Graphs   Utilities   Add-ons   Window   Help

21 : Student   20   Visible: 8 of 8 Variables

	Student	Sex	Age	Quiz1	Quiz2	Quiz3	Quiz4	Quiz5	var
10	10	1	21	86	83	77	64	63	
11	11	1	23	90	71	91	86	87	
12	12	0	18	84	71	67	62	70	
13	13	0	21	83	80	89	60	60	
14	14	0	17	79	77	82	63	74	
15	15	0	19	89	80	64	94	78	
16	16	1	20	76	85	65	92	82	
17	17	1	19	92	76	76	74	91	
18	18	1	22	75	90	78	70	76	
19	19	1	22	87	87	63	73	64	
20	20	0	20	75	74	63	91	87	
21	20	0	20	75	74	63	91	87	
22									
23									

Data View   Variable View

IBM SPSS Statistics Processor is ready

Figure 2-5. *Accidental duplicate entry*

To delete the duplicate record, enter the Data View and then move the mouse pointer into the record number area. You will see that the cursor indicator changes to an arrow. Click the left mouse button to select the row, and then right-click. The following menu will appear (see Figure 2-6).

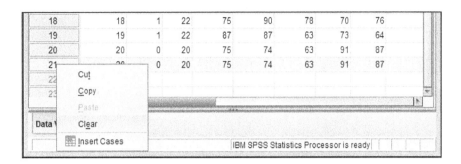

Figure 2-6. *Clearing a data record*

Left-click on **Clear** to delete the duplicate record. You can follow the same approach to delete an unwanted variable by left-clicking in the variable name area. Right-click and you can then delete an unwanted variable by left-clicking **Clear** (see Figure 2-7).

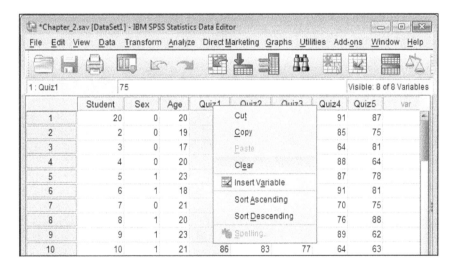

Figure 2-7. *Deleting a variable*

Computing a New Variable

Let us compute a new variable by adding the *Quiz1* and *Quiz2* scores for each student. For this purpose, we use the **Transform** menu in SPSS. SPSS provides a large number of built-in functions and a calculator-like tool for computing new variables.

In this case, we can type in a simple formula and save the total in a new variable called *Sum*. From the SPSS Data Editor, click on **Transform** > **Compute Variable** as shown in Figure 2-8.

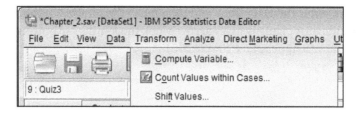

Figure 2-8. *Click on Transform > Compute Variable*

In the resulting dialog box, you can enter the new target variable name and the formula for calculating it (see Figure 2-9). Let us enter our target variable name in the Target Variable window and our simple formula in the Numeric Expression window. We call the new variable *Sum*, and use the simple expression:

$$Quiz1 + Quiz2$$

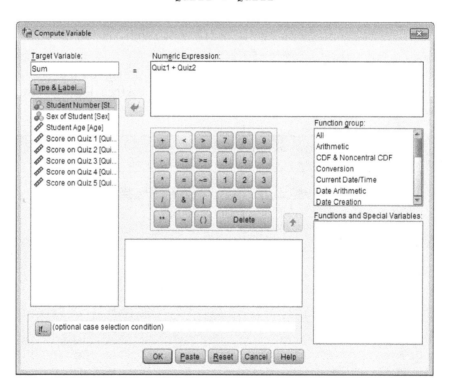

Figure 2-9. *Compute Variable dialog box*

You can type the formula directly, or point and click on the variable names in the left window to enter them in the "Numeric Expression" window. When you are finished with the formula, click **OK**, and the new variable will be calculated and added to the Variable View (Figure 2-10) and the Data View (Figure 2-11).

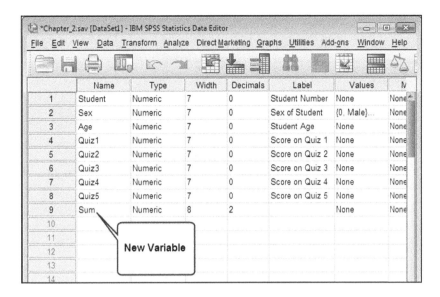

Figure 2-10. *New variable appears in Variable View*

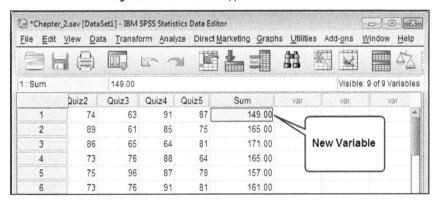

Figure 2-11. *New variable also appears in Data View*

As with most SPSS variables, the computed variable defaults to a numeric type with 8 characters and 2 decimal places. You can modify these settings in the Variable View.

Now let us compute and save a new variable that is the average of all the quizzes. As before, we could use a numeric expression by typing in

```
(Quiz1 + Quiz2 + Quiz3 + Quiz4 + Quiz5)/5
```

(see Figure 2-12). Let us call the new variable *Average*. When we click **OK**, SPSS computes the new variable and adds it to the Data and Variable views of the Data Editor.

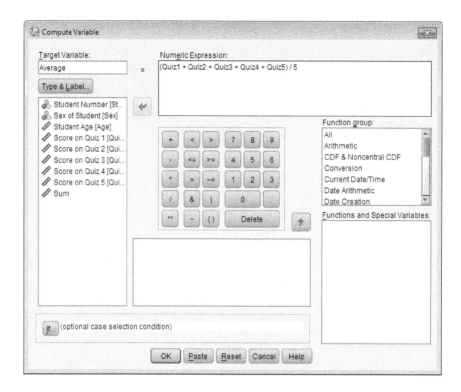

Figure 2-12. *Calculating the average quiz score by use of a formula*

Note the following symbols in the Compute Variable interface, and their functions (see Table 2-2).

Table 2-2. *Compute Variable functions*

Symbol	Function	Symbol	Function	Symbol	Function
+	Add	<	Less than	>	Greater than
-	Subtract	<=	Less than or equal	>=	Greater than or equal
*	Multiply	=	Equals	~=	Not equal
/	Divide	&	And	|	Or
**	Exponent	~	Not	( )	Parentheses

The Compute Variable dialog also gives access to a large number of built-in functions. The same computation we just performed could be more easily accomplished using the built-in function MEAN available through the "Functions and Special Variables" menu. This function is in the Statistical Function group (see Figure 2-13). Delete the *Average* variable you just created, and re-create the variable using the MEAN function.

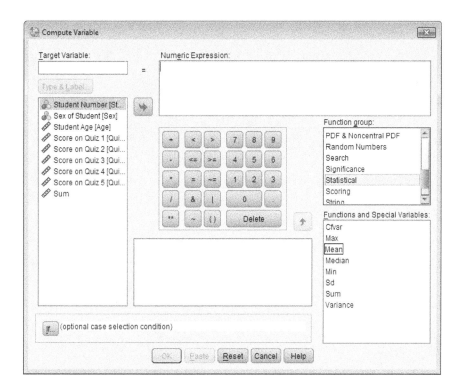

Figure 2-13. *Accessing the built-in statistical functions*

Because the variables *Quiz1* through *Quiz5* occupy adjacent columns in the data set, it is possible to use the "TO" keyword to simplify the numeric expression. Instead of typing each separate variable name, you can type the expression:

```
MEAN(Quiz1 TO Quiz5)
```

As before, you can type this expression directly into the Numeric Expression window, or point to the functions and variable names and click on them to enter the expression. Figure 2-14 shows the simplified expression.

When you click **OK**, SPSS computes the new variable and adds it to the data file (see Figure 2-15). As you have already seen, any newly-created variable will appear in the last row of the Variable View and the last column of the Data View. Save your data file so that you can use it again. Give the file a descriptive name that will help you remember its contents and purpose. We will return to this data set in Chapter 3.

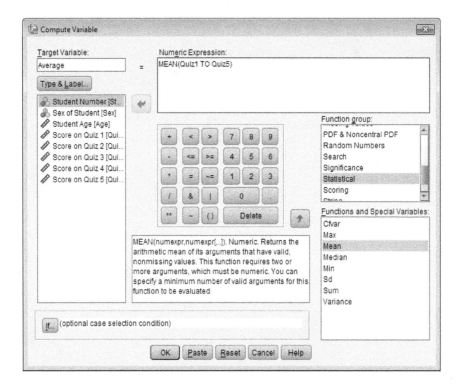

Figure 2-14. Using the Mean function to compute an average

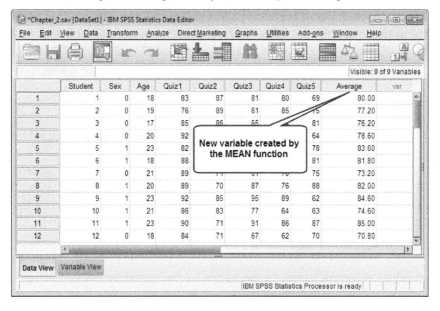

Figure 2-15. New variable created by built-in function

More on Data Handling

Chapter 14 provides instructions on more advanced data handling methods, and includes examples of recoding data and filtering, sorting, splitting, and restructuring SPSS data files.

Chapter 2 Exercises

1. Using the data from this chapter, create a new variable called *Odd* that is the average of the scores on *Quiz1*, *Quiz3*, and *Quiz5*.

2. Using the data from this chapter, create a new variable called *Even* that is the average of the scores on *Quiz2* and *Quiz4*.

3. After completing exercises 1 and 2 above, create a new variable that is the average of the *Odd* and *Even* variables.

4. The following data represent the heights, weights, and class standing of 15 college basketball players. Class standing is 1 (*freshman*), 2 (*sophomore*), 3 (*junior*), and 4 (*senior*). Create an SPSS data file with the appropriate data structure.

Player	Inches	Pounds	Year
1	69	160	1
2	78	200	1
3	79	240	2
4	80	215	1
5	75	200	3
6	81	230	3
7	77	200	3
8	74	185	1
9	77	215	4
10	83	260	2
11	78	205	2
12	77	215	3
13	74	170	1
14	81	220	3
15	76	215	4

Compute a new variable named *Weight* that is the conversion of the player's weight in pounds to kilograms. One kilogram is approximately equal to 2.20 pounds.

5. Using the data from exercise 4 above, compute a new variable named *Height* that is the conversion of the player's height in inches to meters. One meter is approximately equal to 39.37 inches.

6. Using the information from exercises 4 and 5 above, compute a new variable named *BMI* that is the player's body mass index, calculated as the player's weight in kilograms divided by the square of the player's height in meters: $BMI = kg / m^2$.

3 Descriptive Statistics

Objectives

1. Display basic descriptive statistics.
2. Display frequency distributions and graphs.
3. Calculate and save standard scores.

Overview

Descriptive statistics can optionally be included with many statistical procedures, and there are several useful submenus under the **Analyze** > **Descriptive Statistics** menu. Let us use the data set developed in Chapter 2 to examine two of these procedures, the Descriptives and the Frequencies procedures. We will devote Chapter 4 to another descriptive statistics tool called Explore.

Computing and Displaying Basic Descriptive Statistics

Open the data file from the previous chapter in SPSS or retrieve a copy of Chapter_3.sav from the companion web page. To access descriptive statistics, click **Analyze** > **Descriptive Statistics** > **Descriptives** (see Figure 3-1). Figure 3-2 shows the Descriptives dialog.

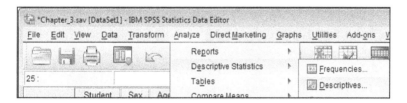

Figure 3-1. *Choose Analyze > Descriptive Statistics > Descriptives*

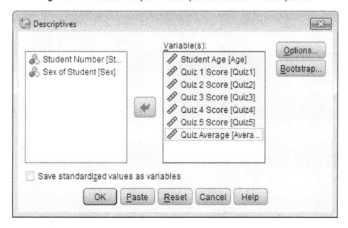

Figure 3-2. *Descriptives dialog*

The Descriptives procedure is suited for interval or ratio (what SPSS calls "scale") variables. In our case, let us ask for statistics for *Age*, all five quiz scores, and the average quiz score. Move the variable names to the Variable(s) list (see Figure 3-2). When you are moving multiple variable names, you can use the **<Ctrl>** key and click on each separate name, or use the **<Shift>** key and then click to select the first and last variables in a consecutive range. Click on **Options** to see the many statistics you can compute and display (see Figure 3-3).

Click **Continue**, and then **OK**. The SPSS Statistics Viewer (see Figure 3-4) displays the requested statistics. Contrary to expectation, you cannot display the mode and median via the Descriptives procedure. You must use the Frequencies procedure for that purpose.

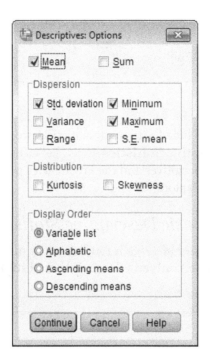

Figure 3-3. *Descriptives Options dialog*

Descriptive Statistics

	N	Minimum	Maximum	Mean	Std. Deviation
Student Age	20	17	23	20.05	1.932
Quiz 1 Score	20	75	92	84.60	5.835
Quiz 2 Score	20	70	90	79.15	6.831
Quiz 3 Score	20	61	96	75.65	11.686
Quiz 4 Score	20	60	94	77.95	11.651
Quiz 5 Score	20	60	91	75.25	9.442
Quiz Average	20	70.80	85.00	78.5200	3.99547
Valid N (listwise)	20				

Figure 3-4. *Descriptive statistics output*

The Frequencies Procedure

The name "Frequencies" is somewhat misleading, because this tool provides summary statistics in addition to frequency tables and several kinds of charts. The Frequencies dialog appears in Figure 3-5. Let us move student *Sex, Age,* the five quiz scores, and the quiz average to the Variable(s) list. Click on the **Statistics** button to see the available options (see Figure 3-6).

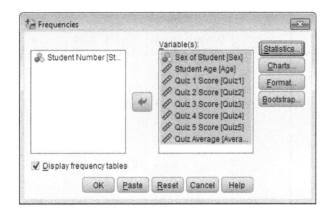

Figure 3-5. Frequencies dialog

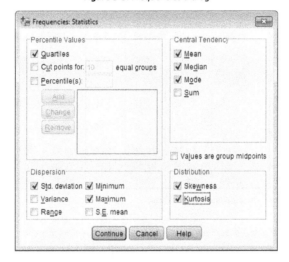

Figure 3-6. Frequencies Statistics dialog

Let us select quartiles, several central tendency measures, and the standard deviation along with other measures of dispersion and distributional shape. Click on **Continue,** and then click the **Charts** button (see Figure 3-7). Select "Histograms" and check "Show normal curve on histogram."

Figure 3-7. Frequencies Charts dialog

Figure 3-8 displays the summary statistics from the SPSS Viewer.

Statistics

		Sex of Student	Student Age	Quiz 1 Score	Quiz 2 Score	Quiz 3 Score	Quiz 4 Score	Quiz 5 Score	Quiz Average
N	Valid	20	20	20	20	20	20	20	20
	Missing	0	0	0	0	0	0	0	0
Mean		.50	20.05	84.60	79.15	75.65	77.95	75.25	78.5200
Std. Error of Mean		.115	.432	1.305	1.527	2.613	2.605	2.111	.89341
Median		.50	20.00	85.50	78.50	76.00	78.00	75.50	78.3000
Mode		0^a	20	89^a	71	76	64^a	64^a	80.00^a
Std. Deviation		.513	1.932	5.835	6.831	11.686	1.16E1	9.442	3.99547
Skewness		.000	.068	-.459	.161	.314	-.165	-.069	-.081
Std. Error of Skewness		.512	.512	.512	.512	.512	.512	.512	.512
Kurtosis		-2.235	-1.010	-1.039	-1.553	-1.172	-1.559	-1.065	-.853
Std. Error of Kurtosis		.992	.992	.992	.992	.992	.992	.992	.992
Minimum		0	17	75	70	61	60	60	70.80
Maximum		1	23	92	90	96	94	91	85.00
Percentiles	25	.00	18.25	79.75	73.00	64.25	65.50	65.25	74.8500
	50	.50	20.00	85.50	78.50	76.00	78.00	75.50	78.3000
	75	1.00	21.75	89.00	85.75	85.75	88.75	81.75	81.8000

a. Multiple modes exist. The smallest value is shown

Figure 3-8. Summary statistics from the Frequencies procedure

Figure 3-9 shows the frequency table for student *Age*. The other variables have similar tables.

Student Age

		Frequency	Percent	Valid Percent	Cumulative Percent
Valid	17	2	10.0	10.0	10.0
	18	3	15.0	15.0	25.0
	19	3	15.0	15.0	40.0
	20	4	20.0	20.0	60.0
	21	3	15.0	15.0	75.0
	22	2	10.0	10.0	85.0
	23	3	15.0	15.0	100.0
	Total	20	100.0	100.0	

Figure 3-9. Frequency table

Figure 3-10 displays the frequency histogram with a superimposed normal curve for student *Age*. Similar charts appear for each variable. In this case. SPSS created a simple frequency histogram. When there are many data points or when the data range is large, SPSS will produce a grouped frequency histogram.

Student Age

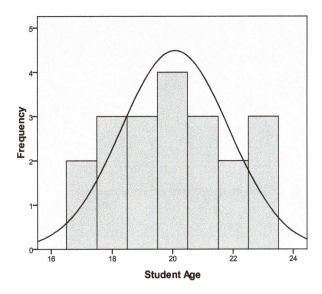

Figure 3-10. Frequency histogram with normal curve

Calculating and Saving Standard Scores

A standard (z) score is a combination statistic that provides information about the location of a given score in the distribution. The z score for a given raw data value shows how far away from the mean the raw score is in standard deviation units as well as whether the score is higher or lower than the mean.

SPSS can easily calculate and save z scores for any continuous variable. We demonstrate with the scores for quiz average. To calculate and save z scores, click **Analyze** > **Descriptive Statistics** > **Descriptives**, and then check the box in front of "Save standardized values as variables" (see Figure 3-11).

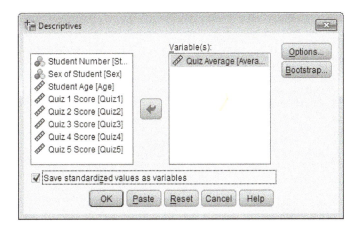

Figure 3-11. Calculating and saving z scores

SPSS calculates and saves the standard scores as a new variable in the data file. The z scores are automatically given a name that begins with Z followed by the original variable name (see Figure 3-12), so the new variable will be called *ZAverage*. Standard scores default to a numeric data type with five decimal places displayed. Of course, you can change the name and the formatting of this new variable if you like.

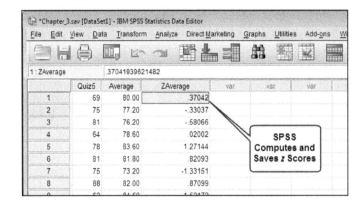

Figure 3-12. *SPSS saves z scores in a new variable*

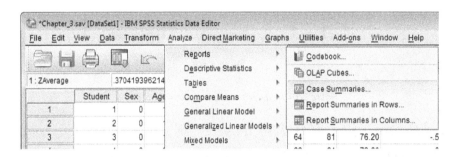

Figure 3-13. *Select Analyze > Reports > Case Summaries*

To display all the *z* scores in the SPSS Viewer, choose **Analyze** > **Reports** > **Case Summaries** (see Figure 3-13). In the resulting dialog, you can specify which variables to summarize. Let us choose *ZAverage* (see Figure 13-4). For demonstration purposes, let us also click on **Statistics** and choose to display the mean and standard deviation to verify that our *z* scores were calculated correctly. If so, the mean will be 0 and the standard deviation 1 by definition, as indeed they are (see Figure 3-15).

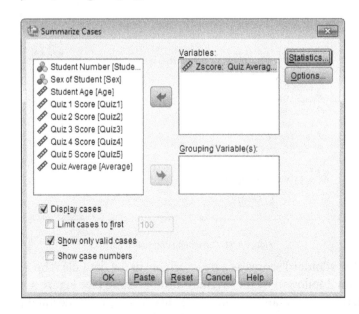

Figure 3-14. *Summarize Cases dialog*

Case Summaries

		Zscore: Quiz Average
1		.37042
2		-.33037
3		-.58066
4		.02002
5		1.27144
6		.82093
7		-1.33151
8		.87099
9		1.52172
10		-.98111
11		1.62184
12		-1.93219
13		-1.03117
14		-.88100
15		.62070
16		.37042
17		.82093
18		-.18020
19		-.93105
20		-.13015
Total	N	20
	Mean	.0000000
	Std. Deviation	1.00000000

Figure 3-15. Case summary output

Chapter 3 Exercises

1. Launch SPSS and click on **Help** > **Tutorial**. Work through the step-by-step tutorial on the time-saving features of SPSS.

2. Compute and save z scores for each of the five quizzes. Use the Case Summaries approach to display the z scores.

3. Using the data from Chapter 2 exercise 4, calculate descriptive statistics for player heights and weights.

4. Use the data from Chapter 2 exercise 4. Use the Frequencies procedure to develop histograms with the normal curve superimposed for player heights and weights. Do player height and weight appear to be normally distributed?

5. Using the data from Chapter 2, exercise 4, calculate and save z scores for player heights and weights. Use the Case Summaries approach to display the z scores.

4 Exploratory Data Analysis

Objectives

1. Perform exploratory data analysis.
2. Examine data distributions using boxplots.
3. Test normality assumptions and examine normal q-q plots.

Overview

You learned in Chapter 3 how to use the Descriptives and Frequencies procedures from the Descriptive Statistics menu. In this chapter you will learn how to use the Explore procedure for exploratory data analysis. We will conduct exploratory data analyses by examining the distributions of the quiz scores for males and females.

The Explore Procedure

Let us conduct an exploratory analysis by selecting *Sex* as the independent or factor variable and *Age* and the various quiz scores as dependent variables. You need not concern yourself with whether these are "dependent" or "independent" variables. You are just telling SPSS the variables to include in the analysis.

To conduct the exploratory analysis, click on **Analyze > Descriptive Statistics > Explore,** as shown in Figure 4-1. In the resulting dialog box, move *Age*, the quiz scores, and the average quiz score into the Dependent List, and move *Sex* into the Factor List (see Figure 4-2).

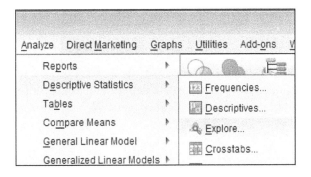

Figure 4-1. *Select Analyze> Descriptive Statistics> Explore*

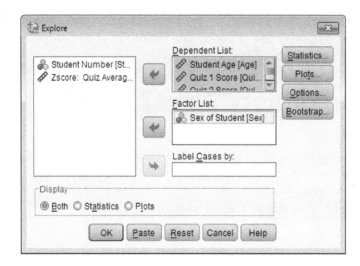

Figure 4-2. Explore dialog

You can display plots, statistics, or both. Click on the **Statistics** button to see the options (see Figure 4-3). Let us choose a 95 percent confidence interval for the mean. Clicking the checkbox for "Outliers" will produce an examination of the extreme values in the data. Outliers also appear as circles outside the fences of the boxplots produced by the Plots dialog. You will see an example of this in Chapter 5.

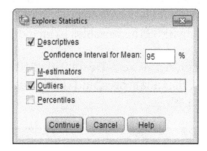

Figure 4-3. Explore statistics dialog

Click on **Continue** and then click on **Plots** (see Figure 4-4). You can choose to display boxplots that compare the dependent variables by the factor(s), or you can group the dependents together in one plot. Let us show the factor levels together and display normality plots with significance tests. We will examine the data distribution to determine whether the normality assumption is met.

Figure 4-4. Explore: Plots dialog

Click on **Continue** to return to the Explore dialog, and then click on **OK**. Figure 4-5 displays the Descriptives table for *Age*, separated by sex, our factor. All the dependent variables have similar tables (not shown).

Descriptives

Sex of Student				Statistic	Std. Error
Student Age	Male	Mean		19.00	.471
		95% Confidence Interval for Mean	Lower Bound	17.93	
			Upper Bound	20.07	
		5% Trimmed Mean		19.00	
		Median		19.00	
		Variance		2.222	
		Std. Deviation		1.491	
		Minimum		17	
		Maximum		21	
		Range		4	
		Interquartile Range		3	
		Skewness		.000	.687
		Kurtosis		-1.334	1.334
	Female	Mean		21.10	.567
		95% Confidence Interval for Mean	Lower Bound	19.82	
			Upper Bound	22.38	
		5% Trimmed Mean		21.17	
		Median		21.50	
		Variance		3.211	
		Std. Deviation		1.792	
		Minimum		18	
		Maximum		23	
		Range		5	
		Interquartile Range		3	
		Skewness		-.475	.687
		Kurtosis		-1.056	1.334

Figure 4-5. Descriptive statistics

Side-by-side boxplots such as those shown for *Age* by *Sex* in Figure 4-6 are very helpful in identifying outliers and in examining distributions. The Kolmogorov-Smirnov and Shapiro-Wilk tests of normality show the significance of any departures from normality (see Figure 4-7). A significant p value would indicate that the data are very unlikely to have a normal distribution. Therefore an insignificant p value would indicate that the data do not depart significantly from a normal distribution. *Quiz1* for females and *Quiz3* for males appear to have some departure from normality, but it is not significant. In this instance you are probably justified in using parametric statistics such as t tests to test hypotheses about sex differences in quiz scores. If the normality tests indicate significant departure from normality, you can try different data transformations to increase the normality of the data or choose nonparametric tests that make few or no distributional assumptions.

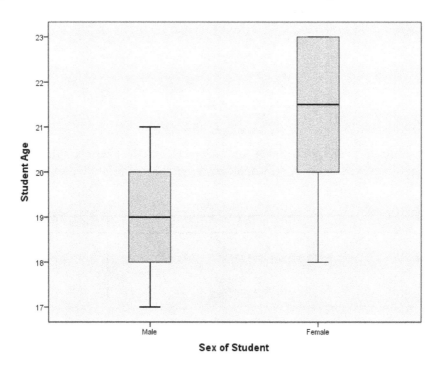

Figure 4-6. *Side-by-side boxplots*

Another very useful way to examine the normality of the data distribution is the normal q-q (quantile-quantile) plot, which plots the expected distribution if the data were normally distributed against the observed values. If the data are normally distributed, there will be a straight-line relationship on the plot. If the data are not normally distributed, the plot will depart from a straight line. Figure 4-8 shows the plot for the average quiz score for males.

Tests of Normality

	Sex of Student	Kolmogorov-Smirnov[a]			Shapiro-Wilk		
		Statistic	df	Sig.	Statistic	df	Sig.
Student Age	Male	.149	10	.200*	.918	10	.341
	Female	.192	10	.200*	.905	10	.246
Quiz 1 Score	Male	.165	10	.200*	.952	10	.694
	Female	.220	10	.189	.869	10	.097
Quiz 2 Score	Male	.162	10	.200*	.908	10	.265
	Female	.185	10	.200*	.910	10	.278
Quiz 3 Score	Male	.249	10	.079	.862	10	.080
	Female	.182	10	.200*	.924	10	.388
Quiz 4 Score	Male	.211	10	.200*	.879	10	.127
	Female	.220	10	.185	.909	10	.272
Quiz 5 Score	Male	.135	10	.200*	.986	10	.989
	Female	.189	10	.200*	.895	10	.193
Quiz Average	Male	.095	10	.200*	.984	10	.983
	Female	.225	10	.162	.898	10	.207

a. Lilliefors Significance Correction
*. This is a lower bound of the true significance.

Figure 4-7. Tests of normality of distribution

The straight-line relationship on the plot is visual confirmation of the results of the normality test for the average quiz variable (see Figure 4-8). The quiz scores of females produced a similar plot (not shown).

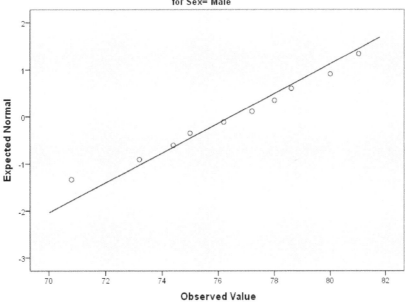

Figure 4-8. Normal q-q plot for quiz average (males)

Chapter 4 Exercises

1. Launch SPSS and open the data file for Chapter 4. Select **Analyze** > **Descriptive Statistics** > **Explore**. Move the *Average* variable to the Dependent List. Leave the factor list empty. Select various statistics and plots and click **OK**. Examine the output.

2. Using the Chapter 4 data file, select **Analyze** > **Descriptive Statistics** > **Explore**. Move all five quiz scores to the Dependent List. Leave the factor list empty. Click on **Plots** and select "Dependents Together" under Boxplots. Click OK. Examine the output. Which of the quizzes is the least variable? Which of the quizzes is the most variable?

3. Use the data from Chapter 2 exercise 4. Conduct an exploratory data analysis of the players' heights and weights.

4. Using the data from Chapter 2 exercise 4, repeat the exploratory data analysis with *Year* as the factor.

5. Launch SPSS. Click on **Help** > **Case Studies**. Click on "Statistics Base" and complete the case study for "Exploratory Data Analysis." You will need to locate the sample files in the Samples subdirectory of the SPSS installation directory on your hard drive.

5

One-Sample *t* Test

Objectives

1. Conduct a one-sample *t* test for a known or hypothesized population mean.
2. Interpret one-sample *t* test results.

Overview

In the one-sample *t* test, we are comparing a sample mean to some known or hypothesized value of the mean in order to determine the likelihood that the sample came from a population with the hypothesized value. We will explore the one-sample *t* test with data for the body temperatures of 130 adults. Let us test the hypothesis that the sample came from a population with a mean temperature of 98.6° Fahrenheit, which is commonly held to be "normal."

Assumptions

For the one-sample *t* test, we assume that the variable being tested comes from a normally distributed population and that the data are at least interval in nature. You learned to test the hypothesis that the data are normally distributed in Chapter 4, and we will repeat that test here for illustrative purposes. With larger sample sizes, the assumption of normality is less important because the sampling distribution of means approaches a normal distribution as sample size increases.

Example Data

In Table 5-1 are the temperature measurements for 130 adults, 65 males and 65 females. These data were published by Dr. Allen Shoemaker of Calvin College and are used with his permission. Reading the data by columns, the first 65 cases are males, and the second 65 are females. The data properly entered in an SPSS file are shown in Figure 5-1. If you like, you may retrieve a copy of the SPSS data file, Chapter_5.sav, from the companion web page for this book.

Table 5-1. Body temperatures for 130 adults

Body Temp				
96.3	98.0	98.7	97.9	98.6
96.7	98.0	98.8	97.9	98.7
96.9	98.0	98.8	98.0	98.7
97.0	98.0	98.8	98.0	98.7
97.1	98.0	98.9	98.0	98.7
97.1	98.1	99.0	98.0	98.7
97.1	98.1	99.0	98.0	98.7
97.2	98.2	99.0	98.1	98.7
97.3	98.2	99.1	98.2	98.8
97.4	98.2	99.2	98.2	98.8
97.4	98.2	99.3	98.2	98.8
97.4	98.3	99.4	98.2	98.8
97.4	98.3	99.5	98.2	98.8
97.5	98.4	96.4	98.2	98.8
97.5	98.4	96.7	98.3	98.9
97.6	98.4	96.8	98.3	99.0
97.6	98.4	97.2	98.3	99.0
97.6	98.5	97.2	98.4	99.1
97.7	98.5	97.4	98.4	99.1
97.8	98.6	97.6	98.4	99.2
97.8	98.6	97.7	98.4	99.2
97.8	98.6	97.7	98.4	99.3
97.8	98.6	97.8	98.5	99.4
97.9	98.6	97.8	98.6	99.9
97.9	98.6	97.8	98.6	100.0
98.0	98.7	97.9	98.6	100.8

Although we are concerned only with the temperatures in this chapter, we will examine possible sex differences in body temperature in the next chapter. In the file Chapter_5.sav, the variable *Sex* is coded 1 (*Male*) and 2 (*Female*).

We will first perform some exploratory data analyses as described in Chapter 4 to test the normality assumption and to examine the data distribution. We will use the Explore menu for this purpose.

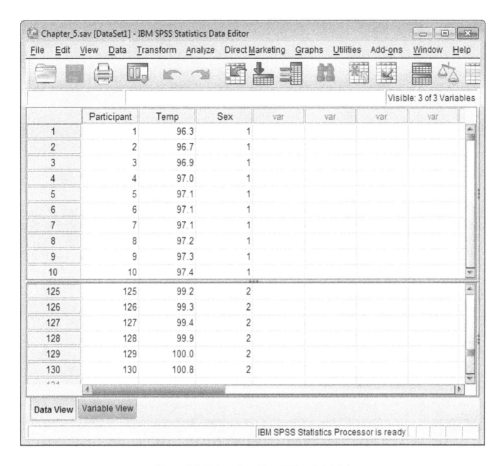

Figure 5-1. *Data entered in SPSS (partial data)*

Exploratory Analysis

Let us examine the distribution and check the assumption of normality. As you know, the most direct way to do that is to use the Explore option under the Descriptive Statistics procedure in the Analyze menu. Select **Analyze** > **Descriptive Statistics** > **Explore** and enter *Temp* in the Dependent List. In the Explore dialogs and menus, select histogram, and normality tests.

The normality test does not indicate a significant departure from normality (see Figure 5-2), and the normal q-q plot indicates few significant deviations from expectation if the data were normally distributed (see Figure 5-3).

Tests of Normality

	Kolmogorov-Smirnov[a]			Shapiro-Wilk		
	Statistic	df	Sig.	Statistic	df	Sig.
Body Temperature	.065	130	.200[*]	.987	130	.233

a. Lilliefors Significance Correction
*. This is a lower bound of the true significance.

Figure 5-2. *Testing the normality assumption*

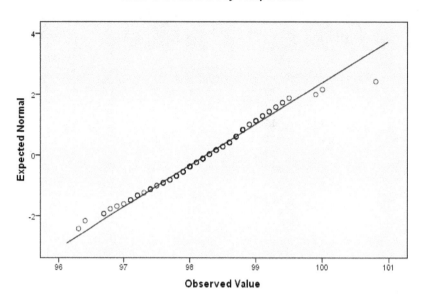

Figure 5-3. Normal q-q plot for body temperature

You can superimpose the normal curve on the histogram of body temperatures for a better visualization of the data. You learned previously how to create a histogram with the normal curve from the Frequencies procedure. You can also do this from the Graphs menu by selecting **Graphs** > **Interactive** or by selecting one of the "legacy" dialogs. We will select **Graphs** > **Legacy Dialogs** > **Histogram** (see Figure 5-4). In the resulting dialog, move *Temp* to the Variable field, and check the box in front of "Display normal curve" (see Figure 5-5). Click on **OK**, and the histogram with normal curve appears (see Figure 5-6).

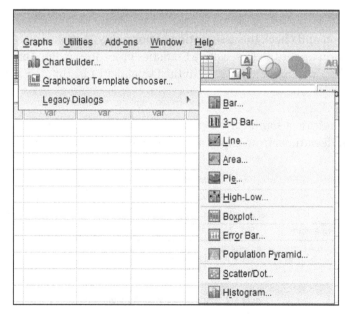

Figure 5-4. Graphs menu

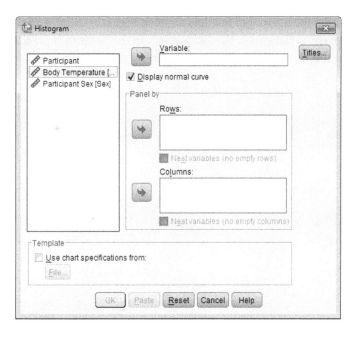

Figure 5-5. Histogram dialog

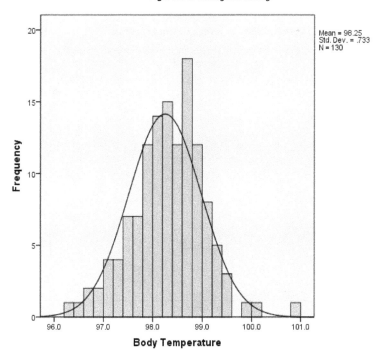

Figure 5-6. Histogram with normal curve

The boxplot created by the Explore procedure (see Figure 5-7) indicates that there are three extreme outliers, which are cases 1, 66, and 130. We might suspect these individuals were not well at the time of testing. If we choose, we can remove these cases by deleting them, filtering them, or recoding the temperature measures for these cases as "system missing" (see Chapter 14 for instructions on how to filter and recode records). Let us simply delete the cases for now as you learned in Chapter 2. You may find it helpful to save a backup copy of your data set when you make such adjustments, in case you want to restore the original data.

After we delete the three records, the normality test has an even higher *p* value, and the new boxplot shows that there are no outliers. The "fences" at the end of the "whiskers" on the boxplot represent 1.5 times the interquartile range (the difference between the first and third quartiles). See Figure 5-8.

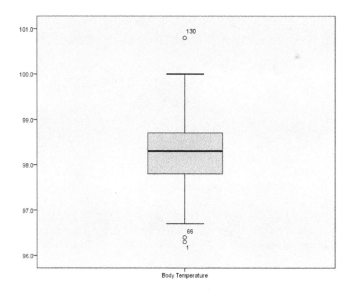

Figure 5-7. *Boxplot showing presence of outliers*

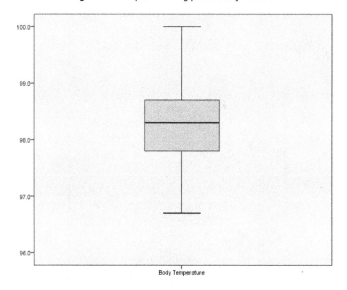

Figure 5-8. *Boxplot after outliers are removed*

Performing the One-Sample t Test

With the preliminary explorations completed, we can now do the one-sample *t* test. To perform the test, select **Analyze > Compare Means, One-Sample T Test**. Move *Temp* to the Test Variables window and enter 98.6 as the test value (see Figure 5-9).

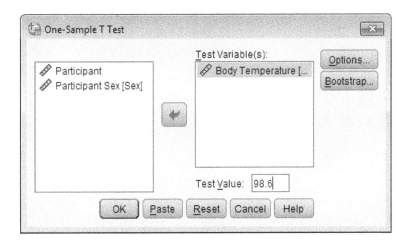

Figure 5-9. One-sample t test dialog

Click **OK** to run the one-sample *t* test procedure. Figure 5-10 shows the *t* test results.

One-Sample Statistics

	N	Mean	Std. Deviation	Std. Error Mean
Body Temperature	127	98.259	.6643	.0589

One-Sample Test

	Test Value = 98.6					
					95% Confidence Interval of the Difference	
	t	df	Sig. (2-tailed)	Mean Difference	Lower	Upper
Body Temperature	-5.784	126	.000	-.3409	-.458	-.224

Figure 5-10. One-sample t test results

The mean body temperature in our sample is 98.259 °F, and the probability that this sample came from a population with a mean temperature of 98.6 °F is less than .001, $t(126) = -5.784$, $p < .001$. As another way to look at this problem, examine the 95% confidence interval of the difference. See that zero (or no difference) is not contained in that interval, indicating that the difference between our sample mean and the hypothesized population mean is significant.

To verify that this significant finding was not the result of removing the outliers, you may choose to reenter those cases and run the analysis again. The results are very similar, and the newly-calculated value of *t* is significant at the .001 level. The widely-held belief that 98.6 °F is the "normal" human body temperature is not true.[1]

---

[1] See Mackowiak, P. A., Wasserman, S. S., & Levine, M. M. (1992). A critical appraisal of 98.6 °F (37 °C), the upper limit of the normal body temperature, and other legacies of Carl Reinhold August Wunderlich. *Journal of the American Medical Association, 12*, 1578-1580.

Chapter 5 Exercises

1. Return to the data from Chapter 1, and conduct one-sample *t* tests for each of the five quizzes, using the test value of 70. What is your conclusion?

2. Use the data from Chapter 2 exercise 4. Conduct a one-sample *t* test for player heights using 74 inches as the test value. What is your conclusion?

3. Using the data from Chapter 2 exercise 4, conduct a one-sample *t* test for player weights using 220 as the test value. What is your conclusion?

4. Launch SPSS. Select **Help** > **Case Studies**. Select "Statistics Base." Complete the Case Study for the "One-Sample T Test." Instructions for splitting the file into groups can be found in Chapter 14.

6

Independent-Samples *t* Test

Objectives

1. Perform an independent-samples *t* test.
2. Interpret independent-samples *t* test results.

Overview

We use the independent-samples *t* test is to compare the means from two separate groups. You need to inform SPSS of group membership by using a separate column to code the group to which a given observation belongs.

Assumptions

For the independent-samples *t* test, we assume that the data come from a normally distributed population, that the measurements in each group are independent of one another, and that the variances of the two groups are equal in the population. As with the one-sample *t* test, the assumption of normality of distribution becomes less important as the sample size increases.

Example Data

We will use the data from the previous chapter to determine whether one sex has a higher temperature than the other sex. For this chapter, the data set has been renamed Chapter_6.sav. The data set includes the body temperatures and a coding variable for sex, 1 (*Female*), 2 (*Male*). See Table 6-1 for the data. If you like, you may retrieve the complete data file, Chapter_6.sav, from the companion web page for this book.

Table 6-1. *Example Data*

Participant	Temp	Sex	Participant	Temp	Sex	Participant	Temp	Sex	Participant	Temp	Sex	Participant	Temp	Sex
1	96.3	1	27	98.0	1	53	98.7	1	79	97.9	2	105	98.6	2
2	96.7	1	28	98.0	1	54	98.8	1	80	97.9	2	106	98.7	2
3	96.9	1	29	98.0	1	55	98.8	1	81	98.0	2	107	98.7	2
4	97.0	1	30	98.0	1	56	98.8	1	82	98.0	2	108	98.7	2
5	97.1	1	31	98.0	1	57	98.9	1	83	98.0	2	109	98.7	2
6	97.1	1	32	98.1	1	58	99.0	1	84	98.0	2	110	98.7	2
7	97.1	1	33	98.1	1	59	99.0	1	85	98.0	2	111	98.7	2
8	97.2	1	34	98.2	1	60	99.0	1	86	98.1	2	112	98.8	2
9	97.3	1	35	98.2	1	61	99.1	1	87	98.2	2	113	98.8	2
10	97.4	1	36	98.2	1	62	99.2	1	88	98.2	2	114	98.8	2
11	97.4	1	37	98.2	1	63	99.3	1	89	98.2	2	115	98.8	2
12	97.4	1	38	98.3	1	64	99.4	1	90	98.2	2	116	98.8	2
13	97.4	1	39	98.3	1	65	99.5	1	91	98.2	2	117	98.8	2
14	97.5	1	40	98.4	1	66	96.4	2	92	98.2	2	118	98.8	2
15	97.5	1	41	98.4	1	67	96.7	2	93	98.3	2	119	98.9	2
16	97.6	1	42	98.4	1	68	96.8	2	94	98.3	2	120	99.0	2
17	97.6	1	43	98.4	1	69	97.2	2	95	98.3	2	121	99.0	2
18	97.6	1	44	98.5	1	70	97.2	2	96	98.4	2	122	99.1	2
19	97.7	1	45	98.5	1	71	97.4	2	97	98.4	2	123	99.1	2
20	97.8	1	46	98.6	1	72	97.6	2	98	98.4	2	124	99.2	2
21	97.8	1	47	98.6	1	73	97.7	2	99	98.4	2	125	99.2	2
22	97.8	1	48	98.6	1	74	97.7	2	100	98.4	2	126	99.3	2
23	97.8	1	49	98.6	1	75	97.8	2	101	98.5	2	127	99.4	2
24	97.9	1	50	98.6	1	76	97.8	2	102	98.6	2	128	99.9	2
25	97.9	1	51	98.6	1	77	97.8	2	103	98.6	2	129	100.0	2
26	98.0	1	52	98.7	1	78	97.9	2	104	98.6	2	130	100.8	2

Performing the Independent-Samples t Test

Because we determined previously that the body temperature measures are roughly normally distributed, we will not repeat that test here. Now, however, we are concerned with another assumption, that of equality of variance, or *homoscedasticity*. We will perform a test of equality of variance as part of the independent-samples *t* test. If the body temperatures for males and females do not have roughly equal variances, we can use a *t* test that considers this inequality by adjusting the degrees of freedom. If the variances are roughly equal, we will perform the standard independent-samples *t* test that assumes the variances are equal.

Access the independent-samples *t* test from the **Analyze** > **Compare Means** menu. Click on **Independent-Samples T test** (see Figure 6-1). Unfortunately, SPSS often labels these as T tests rather than *t* tests, though the labeling is inconsistent. As before, we will exclude cases 1, 66, and 130 from the analysis by deleting or filtering those records.

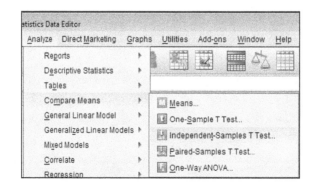

Figure 6-1. *Click Analyze > Compare Means> Independent-Samples T Test*

In the dialog that appears next, enter *Temp* as the Test Variable and *Sex* as the Grouping Variable, as Figure 6-2 shows. The question marks indicate that you must define the groups for *Sex*. Click on the **Define Groups** button.

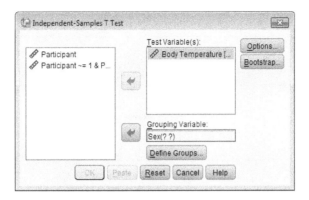

Figure 6-2. Independent-samples t test dialog

In the Define Groups dialog, enter 1 and 2 for the group values (see Figure 6-3). Click on **Continue**, and then click **OK** to conduct the test.

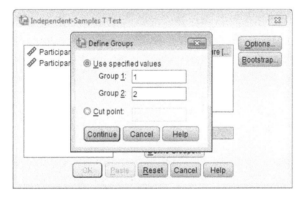

Figure 6-3. Defining groups

The nonsignificant Levene test indicates that we can assume equality of variance and report the values of *t* and *df* corresponding to that assumption. The first table presents the group summary statistics, and the second shows the test results. Our results indicate that females have a significantly higher body temperature than males, $t(125) = -2.191$, $p = .03$ (see Figure 6-4).

Group Statistics

	Participant Sex	N	Mean	Std. Deviation	Std. Error Mean
Body Temperature	Male	64	98.133	.6660	.0832
	Female	63	98.387	.6427	.0810

Independent Samples Test

		Levene's Test for Equality of Variances		t-test for Equality of Means						
									95% Confidence Interval of the Difference	
		F	Sig.	t	df	Sig. (2-tailed)	Mean Difference	Std. Error Difference	Lower	Upper
Body Temperature	Equal variances assumed	.575	.450	-2.191	125	.030	-.2545	.1162	-.4844	-.0246
	Equal variances not assumed			-2.191	124.95	.030	-.2545	.1161	-.4843	-.0247

Figure 6-4. Independent-samples t test results

Chapter 6 Exercises

1. Using the Chapter 6 data, repeat the independent-samples *t* test comparing the body temperatures of males and females with the records for participants 1, 66, and 130 included. Compare the results to those of the test with the records excluded.

2. Return to the data from Chapter 4. Conduct independent-samples *t* tests comparing the ages of males and females and the quiz averages of males and females. Interpret your results.

3. The following data represent scores on a test of mathematical computation. Students were randomly assigned to an experimental method of teaching math and the control method, traditional instruction. Build an appropriate SPSS file using a grouping variable with 0 for the control method and 1 for the experimental method. Conduct an independent-samples *t* test to compare the means of the two groups.

Experimental	Control
91.4	77.5
84.4	70.4
82.1	76.6
78.3	77.0
78.3	77.4
77.5	74.6
81.8	73.8
82.0	79.8
76.5	71.1
86.4	71.4
81.1	80.7
75.4	70.4
82.3	80.4
80.2	

Build an appropriate SPSS data structure and data file. Conduct an independent-samples *t* test comparing the scores of the two groups. What is your conclusion?

4. Launch SPSS. Click **Help** > **Case Studies**. Select "Statistics Base" and work through the case study for the "Independent-Samples T Test" using the sample file.

7

Paired-Samples *t* Test

Objectives

1. Conduct a paired-samples *t* test.
2. Interpret paired-sample *t* test results.

Overview

The paired-samples or dependent *t* test compares the means for two related groups. Many research designs make use of repeated observations for the same cases or participants, such as before and after measures. Other designs use matching on one or more variables to ensure that cases are similar between groups. Still other designs use naturally-occurring pairs such as mothers and daughters, twins, or marriage partners. In all these cases, there is a linkage between the observations for each pair, thus the name paired-samples *t* test.

Assumptions

Because the observations are linked for each pair, the *differences* between the observations are the item of interest in the paired-samples *t* test. We will assume that these differences are normally distributed. If they are not, then data transformations or a nonparametric test would be advisable.

Example Data

Assume that you conducted an experiment to test the Stroop Effect. The computer measures the time in milliseconds it takes participants to identify the color of the text in which a color name word is displayed. For half the stimuli, the displayed color and the color name are congruous. That is, the word "red" is displayed in red and the word "green" is written in green. For the other half of the stimuli, the color name word and the ink color are incongruous. That is, the word "red" might be displayed in green text and the color name "green" might appear in blue text. The participant must press the computer key that identifies the first letter of the actual color of the text, "g" for green, "r" for red, "b" for blue, and so on. The Stroop Effect occurs when the reaction time for incongruous name-color pairings is greater than the reaction time for congruous name-color pairings.

Sixteen participants completed the experiment (data collected by the author). The computer randomized the order of congruous and incongruous pairs and calculated the average reaction time for congruous and incongruous name-color pairs. The example data appear in Table 7-1.

Table 7-1. *Paired-samples data from the Stroop experiment*

Participant	Congruous	Incongruous
1	1240.10	1374.35
2	1256.80	1640.30
3	1649.70	2036.65
4	1454.20	1984.15
5	1110.00	1121.70
6	1353.00	1605.85
7	1123.96	1395.30
8	932.04	1302.88
9	1102.13	1177.73
10	1746.35	1887.60
11	1678.70	2080.25
12	1075.25	1626.70
13	974.15	1477.70
14	896.95	1060.25
15	966.15	1228.60
16	850.90	1280.65

Something is immediately obvious from even a cursory examination of these data. There are large individual differences in reaction times. A key strength of the within-subjects design is that these individual differences are reflected in both measures for a given case, and thus these differences are not allocated to error as they would be in a between-groups design. The data correctly entered in an SPSS file would appear as shown in Figure 7-1.

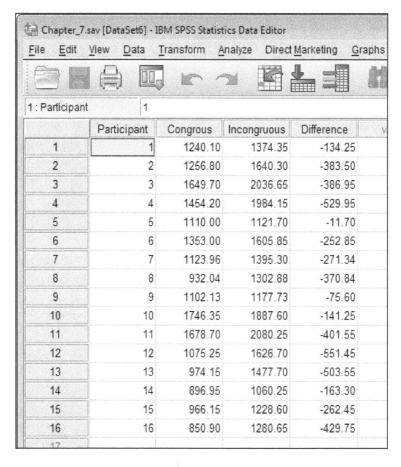

Figure 7-1. *Stroop Effect experiment data in SPSS*

Testing Distributional Assumptions

Let us calculate a new variable called *Difference* by subtracting the reaction time for the congruous condition from the reaction time for the incongruous condition. You learned how to do this in Chapter 2 on working with data, and can go there if you need a refresher. The Compute Variable dialog is shown in Figure 7-2.

Let us examine this new variable to see if we can assume that the differences are normally distributed. As you know, an easy way to do this is to use the **Explore** menu found under **Analyze > Descriptive Statistics**. The normality test and the normal q-q plot for the difference scores indicate that there is not a significant departure of the distribution of the differences from normality (see Figures 7-3 and 7-4), so we can be comfortable using the parametric test. If this distributional assumption is not met, we could try different data transformations or a nonparametric test such as the Wilcoxon matched-pairs signed-ranks test discussed in Chapter 13.

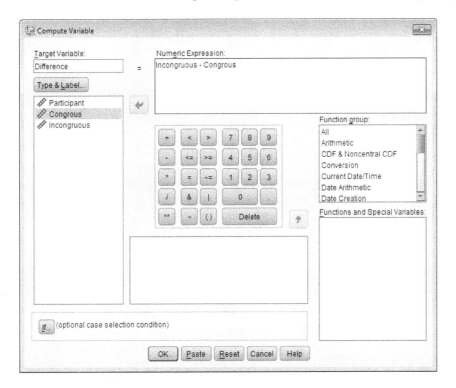

Figure 7-2. *Compute Variable dialog*

Tests of Normality

	Kolmogorov-Smirnov[a]			Shapiro-Wilk		
	Statistic	df	Sig.	Statistic	df	Sig.
Difference	.156	16	.200*	.956	16	.591

*. This is a lower bound of the true significance.

a. Lilliefors Significance Correction

Figure 7-3. *Normality assumption is satisfied*

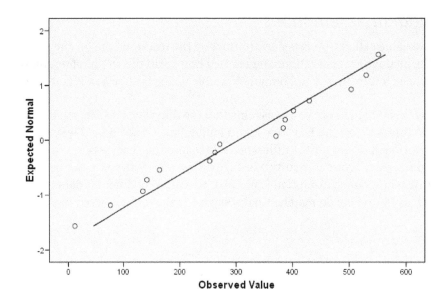

Figure 7-4. Normal q-q plot of difference scores

Performing the Paired-Samples t Test

To perform the paired-samples *t* test, you must inform SPSS which variables are paired. Select **Analyze** > **Compare Means** > **Paired-Samples T Test** (see Figure 7-5). In the resulting dialog, enter *Congruous* and *Incongruous* as the paired variables as shown in Figure 7-6. You must select both names by dragging through them or by clicking on one name and then the other. After highlighting both variable names, click on the arrow to move the pair to the Paired Variables window. You can repeat this process if you have multiple pairings. Click on **OK** to run the paired-samples *t* test.

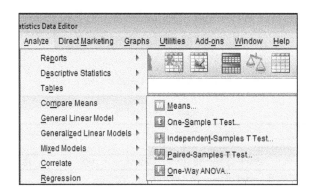

Figure 7-5. Choose Analyze > Compare Means > Paired-Samples T Test

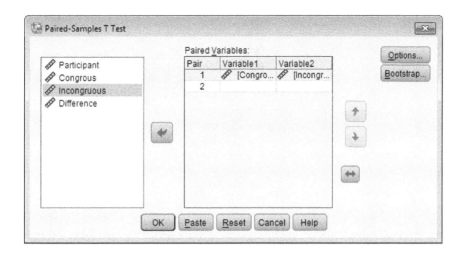

Figure 7-6. *Paired-Samples T Test dialog*

Results indicate that the reaction time for identifying the color of the text was significantly higher for incongruous name-color pairs than for congruous name-color pairs, $t(15) = -7.336$, $p < .001$ (see Figure 7-7).

Paired Samples Statistics

		Mean	N	Std. Deviation	Std. Error Mean
Pair 1	Congrous	1213.1488	16	288.69900	72.17475
	Incongruous	1517.5412	16	334.62030	83.65508

Paired Samples Correlations

		N	Correlation	Sig.
Pair 1	Congrous & Incongruous	16	.868	.000

Paired Samples Test

		Paired Differences							
					95% Confidence Interval of the Difference				
		Mean	Std. Deviation	Std. Error Mean	Lower	Upper	t	df	Sig. (2-tailed)
Pair 1	Congrous - Incongruous	-304.39250	165.97482	41.49370	-392.83424	-215.95076	-7.336	15	.000

Figure 7-7. *Paired-samples t test results*

Chapter 7 Exercises

1. Perform a one-sample *t* test with the data from this chapter. Use the *Difference* variable you created as the dependent variable and a test value of zero (or no difference). Compare your results to those of the paired-samples *t* test discussed in the text. What are your conclusions?

2. The following hypothetical data represent the total calories in a lunch meal purchased by 12 customers at the same fast food restaurant before and after a new calorie-and-nutrition labeling law was passed. Develop an appropriate SPSS data file. Conduct a paired-samples *t* test to determine the effect of the calorie labeling. What is your conclusion?

Before	After
850	796
567	847
672	559
1135	806
992	859
1055	731
603	846
532	470
514	532
738	914
762	517
833	706

3. Using the data from exercise 2 above, calculate a difference score and perform a one-sample *t* test with the test value of zero or no difference. Compare your results to those of the paired-samples *t* test you just performed.

4. The following data represent scores of a group of nine students on a test of statistics knowledge before and after taking a statistics course. The posttest is a parallel version of the pretest. Build an appropriate SPSS data file. Conduct a paired-samples *t* test to determine if the posttest scores are significantly different from the pretest scores. What is your conclusion?

Pretest	Posttest
8	9
12	14
15	15
9	13
11	15
7	12
13	16
10	15
13	16

5. Using the data from exercise 4 above, compute a difference score and use a one-sample *t* test to test the hypothesis that the average difference is zero. Compare the results to those of the paired-samples *t* test.

6. Launch SPSS and complete the case study for the "Paired-Samples T Test" in the Statistics Base menu. You will need the sample file to complete the case study. Using the same data, create new variables by subtracting the final triglyceride score from the initial triglyceride score and by subtracting the final weight from the initial weights. Conduct one-sample *t* tests with the difference scores as your dependent variables and the test value of zero or no difference. Compare the results to those from the paired-samples *t* test.

8

One-Way ANOVA

Objectives

1. Perform a one-way ANOVA.
2. Interpret ANOVA results.
3. Conduct post hoc tests and interpret results.
4. Examine effect size in the one-way ANOVA.

Overview

It is useful to think of the one-way ANOVA as an extension of the independent-samples t test to an overall comparison of three or more means. The one-way ANOVA allows us to conduct a single test to determine whether at least one pair of means differs significantly. If the overall test is significant, we will usually want to perform post hoc or follow-up tests to determine which means are different. You should perform these tests in a way that controls Type I error (rejecting a true null hypothesis). SPSS allows you to perform a one-way ANOVA along with various post hoc comparisons.

Assumptions

Like the independent-samples t test, the ANOVA assumes equality of variance, or homoscedasticity, in the population. ANOVA also assumes that the measurements are independent, are at least at the interval level, and that the variables come from a normally distributed population. When your data violate these assumptions, you could consider data transformations or a nonparametric alternative to the one-way ANOVA such as the Kruskal-Wallis test illustrated in Chapter 13.

Example Data

The following hypothetical data are used to illustrate the one-way ANOVA. Students in a class of 30 are randomly assigned to three different methods of memorizing a 10-word list. Each student practices with the assigned method until he or she can recall all 10 words correctly. A week later, the students are asked to write down as many of the words as they can recall from memory. The data are as follows (see Table 8-1).

Table 8-1. Hypothetical memory method and recall data

Participant	Recall	Method	Participant	Recall	Method	Participant	Recall	Method
1	1	1	11	4	2	21	7	3
2	2	1	12	3	2	22	4	3
3	0	1	13	2	2	23	9	3
4	4	1	14	6	2	24	8	3
5	4	1	15	7	2	25	6	3
6	3	1	16	5	2	26	9	3
7	1	1	17	6	2	27	6	3
8	5	1	18	6	2	28	4	3
9	3	1	19	3	2	29	5	3
10	3	1	20	4	2	30	6	3

These data represent 30 unique individuals and should therefore occupy 30 rows in the SPSS data file. *Recall* is the dependent variable and should occupy one column. The memorization *Method* is the independent variable and should occupy a separate column. The properly configured data in SPSS appear in Figure 8-1.

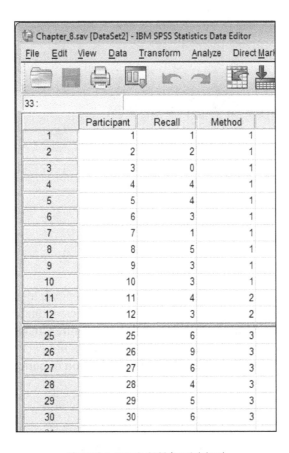

Figure 8-1. Data in SPSS (partial data)

Checking Distributional Assumptions

Type in the data or retrieve Chapter_8.sav from the companion site. Let us first check the normality assumption. Click on **Analyze > Descriptive Statistics > Explore**. From the **Plots** dialog, select "Normality plots with tests" (see Figure 8-2). If the significance level is low (generally .05 or lower) for either the Kolmogorov-Smirnov or Shapiro-Wilk test, you should conclude that the data depart from a normal distribution. In the present case, the results indicate that the data meet the normality assumption (see Figure 8-3). The normal q-q plots show the approximate normal distribution of the recall scores. For illustrative purposes, the normal q-q plot for Method 1 is shown in Figure 8-4. The other two plots are similar.

Figure 8-2. *Select normality plots with tests*

Tests of Normality

		Kolmogorov-Smirnov[a]			Shapiro-Wilk		
	Method	Statistic	df	Sig.	Statistic	df	Sig.
Recall	1	.200	10	.200*	.953	10	.709
	2	.202	10	.200*	.938	10	.532
	3	.186	10	.200*	.917	10	.331

*. This is a lower bound of the true significance.

a. Lilliefors Significance Correction

Figure 8-3. *Normality assumption is satisfied*

Normal Q-Q Plot of Recall

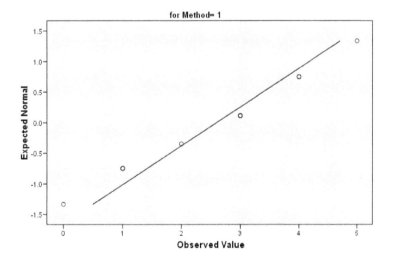

Figure 8-4 Normal q-q plot for Method 1

Performing the One-Way ANOVA

Let us perform the one-way ANOVA and specify a Tukey HSD post hoc test. Click on **Analyze** > **Compare Means** > **One-Way ANOVA** (see Figure 8-5).

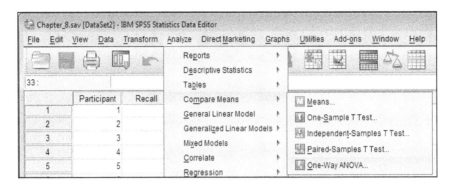

Figure 8-5. Click Analyze > Compare Means > One-Way ANOVA

In the dialog box, indicate the dependent variable (*Recall*) and the factor (levels of the independent variable, *Method*) as Figure 8-6 shows. Click on the **Post Hoc** button and specify the Tukey HSD option (see Figure 8-7). Click on **Continue**.

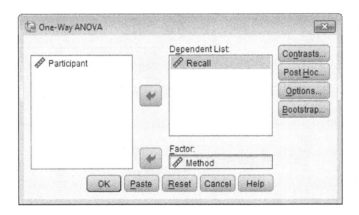

Figure 8-6. One-way ANOVA dialog

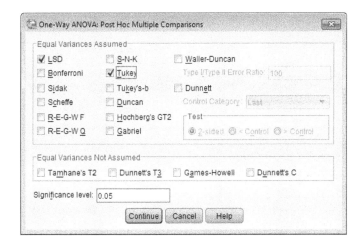

Figure 8-7. *Post Hoc Multiple Comparisons dialog box*

Now click on **Options** and specify the homogeneity of variance test (see Figure 8-8). You can also specify means plots if you desire.

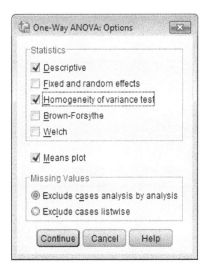

Figure 8-8. *Specifying homogeneity of variance test*

Next, click on **Continue** again and then click on **OK** to run the ANOVA. Figure 8-9 shows the descriptive statistics and the Levene test for homogeneity of variance. The insignificant Levene test indicates that the data meet the assumption of homoscedasticity.

Descriptives

Recall

	N	Mean	Std. Deviation	Std. Error	95% Confidence Interval for Mean Lower Bound	Upper Bound	Minimum	Maximum
1	10	2.60	1.578	.499	1.47	3.73	0	5
2	10	4.60	1.647	.521	3.42	5.78	2	7
3	10	6.40	1.838	.581	5.09	7.71	4	9
Total	30	4.53	2.270	.414	3.69	5.38	0	9

Test of Homogeneity of Variances

Recall

Levene Statistic	df1	df2	Sig.
.142	2	27	.869

Figure 8-9. Homogeneity of variance assumption is satisfied

Interpreting ANOVA Results

The ANOVA summary table and Tukey HSD post hoc comparisons appear in Figures 8-10 and 8-11. The results indicate a significant effect of memorization method on recall. In particular, Methods 2 and 3 produce greater recall than Method 1, but do not differ between themselves.

Recall

	Sum of Squares	df	Mean Square	F	Sig.
Between Groups	72.267	2	36.133	12.637	.000
Within Groups	77.200	27	2.859		
Total	149.467	29			

Figure 8-10. ANOVA summary table

(I) Method	(J) Method	Mean Difference (I-J)	Std. Error	Sig.	95% Confidence Interval Lower Bound	Upper Bound
1	2	-2.000*	.756	.035	-3.87	-.13
	3	-3.800*	.756	.000	-5.67	-1.93
2	1	2.000*	.756	.035	.13	3.87
	3	-1.800	.756	.062	-3.67	.07
3	1	3.800*	.756	.000	1.93	5.67
	2	1.800	.756	.062	-.07	3.67

*. The mean difference is significant at the .05 level.

Figure 8-11. ANOVA post hoc comparison tests (Tukey HSD)

Effect Size in the One-Way ANOVA

Surprisingly, you will not find effect-size indexes in the one-way ANOVA procedure. The most commonly used effect size index for the one-way ANOVA is eta squared (η^2), which is calculated by dividing the between-groups sum of squares by the total sum of squares. In our current case, $\eta^2 = 72.267/149.467 = .483$. Although calculating η^2 is simple enough, the Means procedure found under **Analyze > Compare Means > Means** (see Figure 8-12) provides an alternative approach that allows the user to produce an ANOVA table *and* the value of η^2. In the Means dialog, identify the dependent and independent variable, and then check "ANOVA table and eta" under **Options**. Note the equivalence of the ANOVA tables from the One-Way and Means procedures (see Figure 8-13).

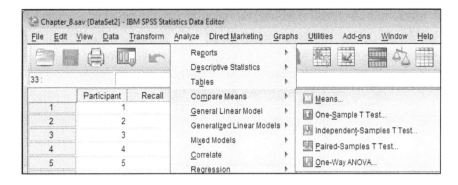

Figure 8-12. Select Analyze > Compare Means > Means

			Sum of Squares	Mean Square	F	Sig.
Recall * Method	Between Groups	(Combined)	72.267	36.133	12.637	.000
	Within Groups		77.200	2.859		
	Total		149.467			

Measures of Association

	Eta	Eta Squared
Recall * Method	.695	.483

Figure 8-13. ANOVA table and eta-squared computed by Means procedure

Chapter 8 Exercises

1. The fleet manager of a delivery service randomly assigned 15 identical new fuel-efficient delivery trucks to three groups of five each. Each vehicle was tested at 55 MPH for 400 highway miles using gasoline Brand A, Brand B, or Brand C. Gasoline mileage for was recorded in miles per gallon. The results were as follows:

BrandA	BrandB	BrandC
34.0	35.3	33.3
35.0	36.5	34.0
34.3	36.4	34.7
35.5	37.0	33.0
35.8	37.6	34.9

Build an appropriate SPSS data file. Conduct a one-way ANOVA comparing the mean mileage for the three brands. Use an alpha level of .05. What is the value of eta squared? If the overall F-ratio is significant, conduct a Tukey HSD test to determine which pairs of means are significantly different at an experiment-wise alpha level of .05. Assuming that the gasoline brands are all priced the same, what brand of gasoline should the fleet manager purchase?

2. The fleet manager wants to purchase new cars, and finds the following information concerning overall (combined highway and city) gasoline mileage for subcompact cars different manufacturers (source: www.consumerreports.org). Build an appropriate SPSS data file. Conduct a one-way ANOVA comparing the gasoline mileage of the cars from the five different manufacturers. Use an alpha level of .05. What is the value of eta squared? If the overall F-ratio is significant, conduct a Tukey HSD test to determine which pairs of means are significantly different at an experiment-wise alpha level of .05. On the basis of

your analysis, which manufacturer(s) would you recommend if the goal is to achieve the highest average gasoline mileage?

Honda	Kia	Chevy	Hyundai	Toyota
28	25	24	27	32
37	28	25	27	33
31	28	28	28	34
32	30	27	30	
34				

3. Twenty-two workers were randomly assigned to three groups. Participants completed a simple puzzle-solving task while listening to music they liked, music they disliked, or no music. The dependent variable is the number of seconds to complete the puzzle. The hypothetical data are as follows.

Like	Dislike	None
67	68	65
60	64	60
71	71	68
57	76	66
58	76	75
59	79	70
57	59	70
	69	

Build an appropriate SPSS data file. Conduct a one-way ANOVA comparing the three groups. Use an alpha level of .05. What is the value of eta squared? If the overall F-ratio is significant, conduct a Tukey HSD test to determine which pairs of means are significantly different at an experiment-wise alpha level of .05. What are your conclusions?

4. Fifteen participants were randomly assigned to three groups. Each individual entered numerical information using one of three panels (A, B, or C). The data are the number of data entry errors. The hypothetical data are below.

PanelA	PanelB	PanelC
0	6	6
4	7	4
1	4	3
0	2	1
2	4	3

Build an appropriate SPSS data file. Conduct a one-way ANOVA comparing the three groups. Use an alpha level of .05. What is the value of eta squared? If the overall F-ratio is significant, conduct a Tukey HSD test to determine which pairs of means are significantly different at an experiment-wise alpha level of .05. What are your conclusions?

5. Launch SPSS. Select **Help** > **Case Studies**. Select "Statistics Base," and work through the case study for "One-Way Analysis of Variance."

9

Repeated-Measures ANOVA

Objectives

1. Perform repeated-measures ANOVA.
2. Interpret ANOVA results.
3. Examine effect size.
4. Conduct post hoc tests and interpret results.
5. Conduct repeated-measures ANOVA using SPSS Base version.

Overview

The repeated-measures or within-subjects ANOVA is used when there are more than two measurements for the same case or participant. We partition the total sum of squares into three components, a between-groups or treatment sum of squares, a within-subjects sum of squares, and a residual or error sum of squares. In this design, each case serves as its own control, so that variance attributable to individual differences is now considered systematic rather than an error term. For this reason, the repeated-measures ANOVA is a generally more powerful test than the between-groups ANOVA.

The repeated-measures ANOVA requires the SPSS Advanced Models add-on. For those without access to the Advanced Models, it is possible to use the Base version of SPSS to perform the repeated-measures analysis as a special case of two-way ANOVA, as illustrated at the end of this chapter.

Conceptually, the repeated-measures ANOVA is an extension of the paired-samples *t* test to three or more measurements. In this book we will examine a simple case, four repeated measures for each participant. It is possible to have a mixed design in which one or more factors are within-subjects and one or more factors are between-groups variables. SPSS is capable of handling these mixed designs, but that topic is beyond the scope of this basic text.

The repeated-measures ANOVA makes assumptions similar to those of the one-way ANOVA. The measures are assumed to be interval or ratio in nature, with equal population variances, and sampled from a normally distributed population. The data are not independent, because the repeated measures are from the same subjects. There is an additional assumption regarding the pattern of the variances and covariances of the repeated measures. This is the assumption of sphericity, which SPSS tests automatically for repeated-measures ANOVA. When your data violate these underlying assumptions, a good nonparametric alternative to the repeated-measures ANOVA is the Friedman test available in SPSS.

Example Data

Five individuals performed a simple reaction time task after taking each of four drugs. The order of the drugs was randomized for each participant. The hypothetical data are as follows (see Table 9-1). You may retrieve the data file, Chapter_9.sav, from the book's companion web site.

Table 9-1. *Hypothetical repeated-measures data*

	Drug1	Drug2	Drug3	Drug4
Person1	30	28	16	34
Person2	14	18	10	22
Person3	24	20	18	30
Person4	38	34	20	44
Person5	26	28	14	30

If the Advanced Models add-on is installed, the Repeated Measures option will be found under **Analyze > General Linear Models**. If you do not have Advanced Models, you can still perform the repeated-measures ANOVA, as illustrated later in this chapter.

The data file should appear as shown in Figure 9-1. These data are in "wide" format with a row for each participant and a separate column for each repeated measure.

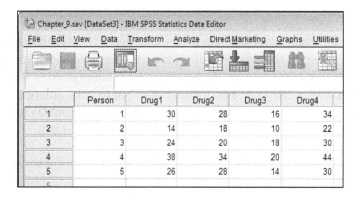

Figure 9-1. *SPSS data file for hypothetical drug data*

Checking Distributional Assumptions

Using the same procedure described in the previous chapter, we will test the normality of the distribution of the four reaction time scores. Chapter 8 explains and illustrates these steps if you need a refresher. Results indicate that the distributions of the four scores do not deviate significantly from normal (see Figure 9-2).

Tests of Normality

	Kolmogorov-Smirnov[a]			Shapiro-Wilk		
	Statistic	df	Sig.	Statistic	df	Sig.
Drug1	.192	5	.200*	.985	5	.962
Drug2	.243	5	.200*	.922	5	.544
Drug3	.141	5	.200*	.979	5	.928
Drug4	.201	5	.200*	.949	5	.731

a. Lilliefors Significance Correction
*. This is a lower bound of the true significance.

Figure 9-2. *Tests show normality assumption is met*

SPSS performs the Mauchly sphericity test automatically when you choose the repeated measures option. If this test is significant, you cannot assume sphericity, and you should use the multivariate test reporting Wilks Lambda. Alternatively, you can adjust the degrees of freedom for the univariate F using the correction factor labeled "epsilon." SPSS shows the values of epsilon and the adjusted degrees of freedom. If the sphericity test is not significant, this indicates that the data meet the assumption of sphericity, and the univariate test for the within-subjects factor can be interpreted without adjustment. In the current case, the insignificant chi-square value associated with the Mauchly W statistic indicates that the sphericity assumption is satisfied (see Figure 9-3).

Mauchly's Test of Sphericity^b

Measure:MEASURE_1

Within Subjects Effect	Mauchly's W	Approx. Chi-Square	df	Sig.	Epsilon^a		
					Greenhouse-Geisser	Huynh-Feldt	Lower-bound
factor1	.186	4.572	5	.495	.605	1.000	.333

Tests the null hypothesis that the error covariance matrix of the orthonormalized transformed dependent variables is proportional to an identity matrix.

a. May be used to adjust the degrees of freedom for the averaged tests of significance. Corrected tests are displayed in the Tests of Within-Subjects Effects table.
b. Design: Intercept
  Within Subjects Design: factor1

Figure 9-3. Sphericity test results

Pairwise Comparisons in Repeated-Measures ANOVA

Although the repeated-measures procedure does not allow directly for post hoc comparisons for within-subjects factors, it is possible to perform these in two different but equivalent ways. You can simply perform paired-samples t tests and use a "Bonferroni correction" to protect the overall alpha (probability of Type I error) level. This involves dividing the nominal alpha level for the overall F test by the number of comparisons for a new alpha level. For example with four groups there are six pairwise comparisons, so the alpha level for each pairwise comparison would be set to .05/6 = .0083. As an equivalent procedure, you can choose to compare main effects and have SPSS make the Bonferroni correction. We will illustrate the second approach.

Performing the Repeated-Measures ANOVA

With the background issues out of the way, we can now perform the repeated-measures ANOVA. Click on **Analyze > General Linear Model > Repeated Measures** (see Figure 9-4).

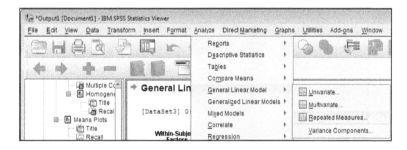

Figure 9-4. Click Analyze> General Linear Model > Repeated Measures

In the dialog box, you must specify the number of repeated measures and the variables that represent the levels of the measurement. Let us label the factor *drug* and indicate that there are four levels (see Figure 9-5).

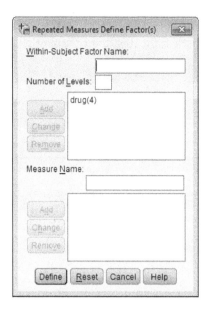

Figure 9-5. *Repeated Measures Define Factor(s) dialog*

Now click on **Add** and then click on **Define** to indicate the variables that are included as the four levels (see Figure 9-6).

In this case, we have only one factor so we will stay in the Repeated Measures dialog to specify the contrasts we need. Click on **Options** and then move *Time* to the "Display Means for" window (see Figure 9.7).

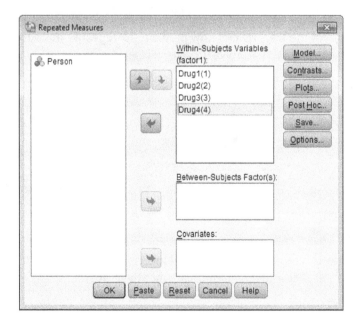

Figure 9-6. *Repeated Measures dialog*

In the repeated-measures ANOVA, SPSS reports "partial eta-squared" as the measure of effect size (see Figure 9-7).

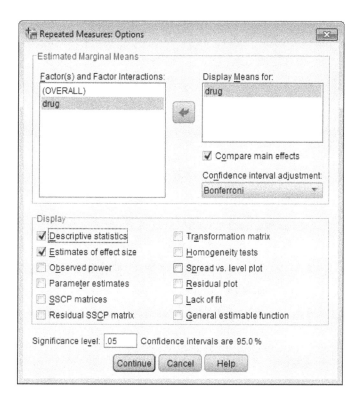

Figure 9-7. Repeated Measures Options

The Post Hoc menu options are grayed out in the Repeated Measures dialog, but you can achieve the same goal by selecting "Compare main effects" in the Repeated Measures Options dialog (see Figure 9-7). To control for Type I error, specify the Bonferroni adjustment in the "Confidence interval adjustment" dropdown. If you like, you can also check the boxes for descriptive statistics and estimates of effect size.

You may also want to click on **Plots** and select to show a plot for the levels of *drug*. To do so, click on *drug*, move it to the Horizontal axis, and then click **Add** (see Figure 9-8) to move the factor to the Plots window.

Now that you have specified your repeated-measures ANOVA including pairwise comparisons and plots, you can click on **Continue** and then **OK** to run the procedure.

Figure 9-8. Specifying profile plots for drug

As we established earlier that the data meet the sphericity assumption, we will not repeat that discussion here, except to point out that we will report the univariate F ratio and degrees of freedom matching that assumption (see Figure 9-9). Our test indicates that reaction time is affected by the drug taken, $F(3, 12) = 24.76$, $p < .001$, partial $\eta^2 = .86$.

Tests of Within-Subjects Effects

Measure:MEASURE_1

Source		Type III Sum of Squares	df	Mean Square	F	Sig.	Partial Eta Squared
drug	Sphericity Assumed	698.200	3	232.733	24.759	.000	.861
	Greenhouse-Geisser	698.200	1.815	384.763	24.759	.001	.861
	Huynh-Feldt	698.200	3.000	232.733	24.759	.000	.861
	Lower-bound	698.200	1.000	698.200	24.759	.008	.861
Error(drug)	Sphericity Assumed	112.800	12	9.400			
	Greenhouse-Geisser	112.800	7.258	15.540			
	Huynh-Feldt	112.800	12.000	9.400			
	Lower-bound	112.800	4.000	28.200			

Figure 9-9. Repeated-measures ANOVA results

The Bonferroni-corrected pairwise comparisons appear in Figure 9-10. Results indicate that the reaction time means for Drugs 1 and 4 are different and that the reaction time means for Drugs 3 and 4 are different.

Pairwise Comparisons

Measure:MEASURE_1

(I) drug	(J) drug	Mean Difference (I-J)	Std. Error	Sig.ª	95% Confidence Interval for Differenceª	
					Lower Bound	Upper Bound
1	2	.800	1.625	1.000	-7.082	8.682
	3	10.800	2.577	.083	-1.700	23.300
	4	-5.600*	.748	.010	-9.230	-1.970
2	1	-.800	1.625	1.000	-8.682	7.082
	3	10.000	2.280	.071	-1.062	21.062
	4	-6.400	1.600	.097	-14.162	1.362
3	1	-10.800	2.577	.083	-23.300	1.700
	2	-10.000	2.280	.071	-21.062	1.062
	4	-16.400*	2.227	.011	-27.204	-5.596
4	1	5.600*	.748	.010	1.970	9.230
	2	6.400	1.600	.097	-1.362	14.162
	3	16.400*	2.227	.011	5.596	27.204

Based on estimated marginal means

a. Adjustment for multiple comparisons: Bonferroni.

*. The mean difference is significant at the .05 level.

Figure 9-10. Pairwise comparison results

The profile plot shows the means for the four drugs and can assist in interpreting the comparisons (see Figure 9-11).

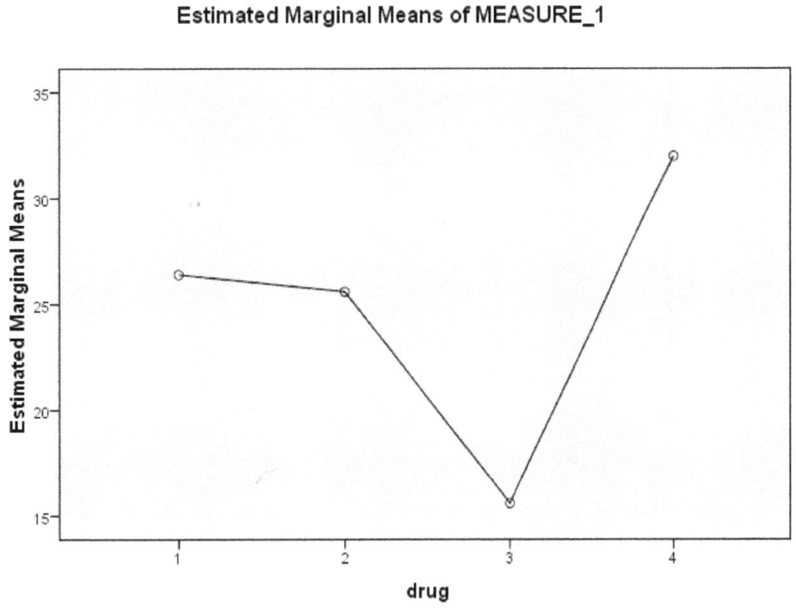

Estimated Marginal Means of MEASURE_1

Figure 9-11. Plot of repeated measures

Repeated-Measures Alternate Approach

Many students and researchers have access only to the Base version of SPSS, and that version does not include the **Analyze** > **General Linear Model** > **Repeated Measures** option. It is still possible to do a repeated-measures ANOVA, but doing so requires rearranging the data file so that the subject or participant number is treated as a random factor. We can then use the **Analyze > General Linear Model > Univariate** menu in the base version of SPSS and treat the repeated-measures ANOVA as a special case of the two-way ANOVA with one observation per cell. This requires suspending the general rule provided earlier that there should be only one row for each participant or subject. We will explore this alternate approach with the same data set we have been using for this chapter.

We must reorganize the data to include columns for the participant number, the condition, and the dependent variable. To accomplish this, we will need to perform minor surgery on the previous data set. In the column labeled Person, the participant number is repeated 4 times. Instead of the previous *Drug1*, *Drug2*, *Drug3*, and *Drug4* columns, we now use an index variable we can call *Drug*, which is coded 1, 2, 3, and 4. Enter the dependent variable, which is the reaction time score, in a single column labeled *Score*. See Figure 9-12 for the proper layout of the reconfigured data file.

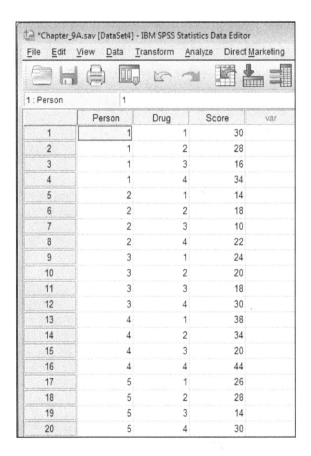

Figure 9-12. Data rearranged for repeated-measures ANOVA using SPSS Base version

With such a small data set, these rearrangements are not very difficult, but SPSS provides a wizard for restructuring data from "wide" to "long" format or vice versa. This wizard is very helpful for larger data sets. For instructions on how to restructure these data in SPSS using the **Data > Restructure** menu, see Chapter 14.

After you reorganize the data, you can use the Base version of SPSS and perform the repeated-measures ANOVA. To do this, select **Analyze > General Linear Model > Univariate** as shown in Figure 9-13. Then in the resulting dialog, move *Score* to the Dependent Variable field, *Drug* to the Fixed Factor(s) field, and *Person* to the Random Factor(s) field (see Figure 9-14). When you click **OK**, SPSS will compute the equivalent of a repeated-measures ANOVA. The *F* ratio of interest is the one for "Hypothesis" for *Drug* in the "Tests of Between-Subjects

Effects table" (see Figure 9-15). Note that this *F* ratio is identical to the one for the within-subjects factor shown previously in Figure 9-9.

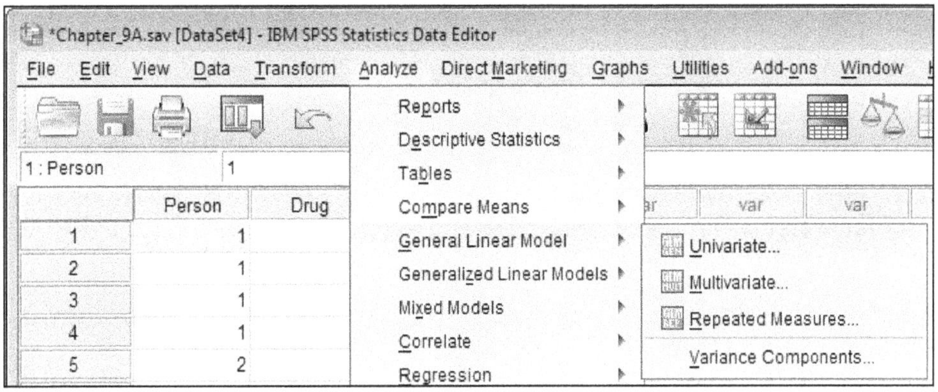

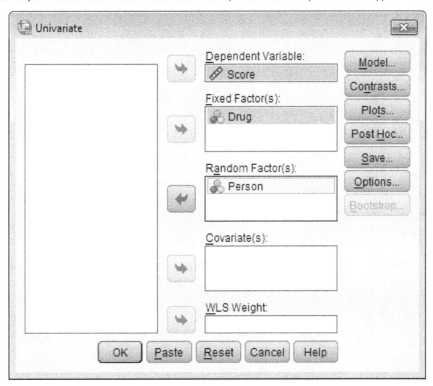

Figure 9-13. *Select Analyze > General Linear Model > Univariate. The Repeated Measures option does not appear in the SPSS Base version.*

Figure 9-14. *In the Univariate dialog, enter Person as a random factor*

Tests of Between-Subjects Effects

Dependent Variable:Score

Source		Type III Sum of Squares	df	Mean Square	F	Sig.
Intercept	Hypothesis	12400.200	1	12400.200	72.857	.001
	Error	680.800	4	170.200[a]		
Drug	Hypothesis	698.200	3	232.733	24.759	.000
	Error	112.800	12	9.400[b]		
Person	Hypothesis	680.800	4	170.200	18.106	.000
	Error	112.800	12	9.400[b]		
Drug * Person	Hypothesis	112.800	12	9.400	.	.
	Error	.000	0	.[c]		

a. MS(Person)

b. MS(Drug * Person)

c. MS(Error)

Figure 9-15. *Repeated-measures ANOVA results from SPSS Base version*

Chapter 9 Exercises

1. A researcher is interested in comparing three different methods of measuring responses to a specific visual stimulus. Each technique yields a score on a 1 – 5 scale. Five students serve as participants, and the same stimulus is presented to each student in three separate trials. The data are as shown below.

	Method1	Method2	Method3
Student1	1	1	2
Student2	2	2	3
Student3	4	3	4
Student4	3	4	5
Student5	4	5	5

Build an appropriate SPSS data file. Conduct and interpret a repeated-measures ANOVA. If there is a significant overall F ratio, use Bonferroni-corrected comparisons to determine which means differ significantly from one another.

2. Repeat the analysis in exercise 1 above using the alternate approach with the **General Linear Model > Univariate** procedure. Compare the results of the two analyses.

3. Three lists, each containing 35 pairs of words, were presented in a randomly chosen order to each of eight participants. The data are the number of pairs correctly recalled for each list. The data are as follows:

	List1	List2	List3
Person1	22	15	18
Person2	15	9	12
Person3	16	13	10
Person4	19	9	10
Person5	20	12	13
Person6	17	14	12
Person7	14	13	10
Person8	17	19	18

Build an appropriate SPSS data file. Conduct and interpret a repeated-measures ANOVA. Are the lists equally difficult? If there is a significant overall F ratio, use Bonferroni-corrected comparisons to determine which means differ significantly from one another.

4. Repeat the analysis in exercise 1 above using the alternate approach with the **General Linear Model >
    Univariate** procedure. Compare the results of the two analyses.

10 Two-Way ANOVA

Objectives

1. Perform a two-way ANOVA.
2. Examine main effects and interaction effects.
3. Examine effect sizes.
4. Plot cell means.

Overview

In the two-way ANOVA, there are two independent variables, each of which has at least two levels. The simplest two-way design is a completely-crossed balanced factorial design. Each cell in the two-way table has the same number of observations, and represents an independent group of observations. The independent variables are thus between-groups factors. The two-way ANOVA is an efficient and economical design because it allows the researcher to examine main effects for each independent variable separately, as well as to examine the possible interaction of the two variables.

Example Data

Assume that you are studying the effects of observing violent acts on subsequent aggressive behavior. You are interested in the kind of violence observed: a violent cartoon versus a video of real-action violence. A second factor is the amount of time one is exposed to violence: ten minutes or 30 minutes. You randomly assign eight children to each group. After watching the violent cartoon or action video, the participant plays a Tetris-like computer video game for 30 minutes. The game provides options for either aggressing ("trashing" the other computerized player) or simply playing for points without interfering with the other player. The program provides 100 opportunities for the player to make an aggressive choice and records the number of times the participant chooses an aggressive action when the game provides the choice. The hypothetical data are as follows (see Figure 10-1).

| | | Type of Violence | |
		Cartoon	Real-Action
Time of Exposure	10 Min.	47	52
		56	62
		48	57
		51	49
		46	64
		44	39
		50	50
		51	48
	30 Min.	67	81
		69	92
		65	82
		62	92
		67	82
		69	94
		59	86
		72	83

Figure 10-1. Hypothetical data

It should be clear that the 32 observations represent 32 unique individuals, and that the data should be coded and entered in SPSS in such a way that the kind of violence and the amount of time watching are entered in separate columns. We used 1 and 2 to indicate the levels of the independent variables, but you could just as easily use 0 and 1. It is a good idea as always to use variable and value labels to clarify the reporting and interpretation of the results.

The dependent variable is the frequency of aggressive behavior. Examine Figure 10-2 to view a portion of the properly coded and entered data. Figure 10-3 shows the Variable View of the data. This data set is available at the companion web page.

We will use the General Linear Model's Univariate procedure to conduct the two-way ANOVA.

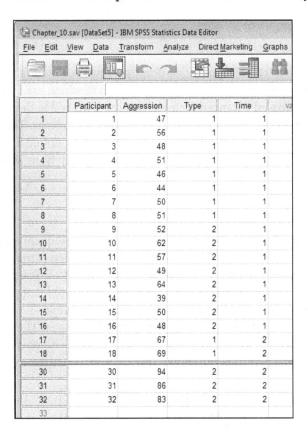

Figure 10-2. Properly coded data for two-way ANOVA (partial data)

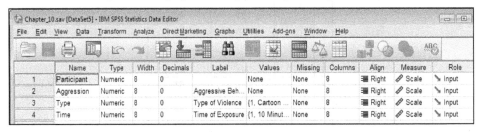

Figure 10-3. Variable View

Checking Distributional Assumptions

The two-way ANOVA assumes homoscedasticity and normality. We can test the normality assumption using the **Analyze** > **Descriptive Statistics** > **Explore** menu. Test results indicate that the aggression measures do not depart significantly from normal for either factor (type of violence or time of exposure to violence). See Figure 10-4. As we have demonstrated previously, normal q-q plots are also helpful in making this determination, though they are not shown here. The homogeneity assumption can be tested via the Options menu in the Univariate dialog box. The test performed is Levene's test.

Tests of Normality

	Type of Violence	Kolmogorov-Smirnov[a]			Shapiro-Wilk		
		Statistic	df	Sig.	Statistic	df	Sig.
Aggressive Behavior	Cartoon Violence	.194	16	.111	.907	16	.106
	Real Violence	.229	16	.024	.896	16	.070

a. Lilliefors Significance Correction

Tests of Normality

	Time of Exposure	Kolmogorov-Smirnov[a]			Shapiro-Wilk		
		Statistic	df	Sig.	Statistic	df	Sig.
Aggressive Behavior	10 Minutes	.180	16	.175	.951	16	.506
	30 Minutes	.178	16	.187	.926	16	.213

a. Lilliefors Significance Correction

Figure 10-4. Normality assumption is met

Performing the Two-Way ANOVA

To perform the two-way ANOVA, click on **Analyze** > **General Linear Model** > **Univariate** (see Figure 10-5). In the resulting dialog box, move *Aggression* to the Dependent Variable window, and *Type* and *Time* to the Fixed Factor(s) window (see Figure 10-6).

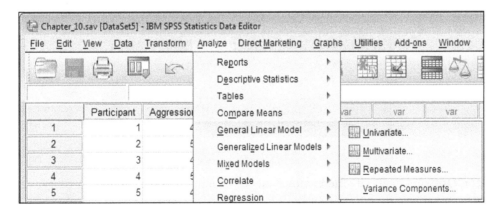

Figure 10-5. Click Analyze > General Linear Model > Univariate

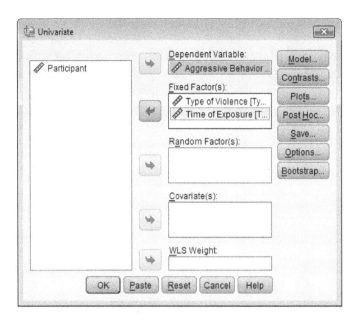

Figure 10-6. *Univariate dialog box*

Because there are only two levels of each factor, post hoc comparisons are not necessary. You can click on **Plots** to display plots of the cell means for each of the four groups. In the Plots dialog, move *Time* to the Horizontal Axis, and *Type* to Separate Lines. Then click on **Add** to select this plot (see Figure 10-7).

Figure 10-7. *Profile Plots dialog*

We will also click on **Options** to specify the homogeneity of variance test (see Figure 10-8). We can also choose descriptive statistics and effect size estimates from this menu.

Figure 10-8. *Options dialog*

Now click on **Continue**, and then click **OK** to run the two-way ANOVA. The descriptive statistics and homogeneity test are shown in Figure 10-9. Results indicate that the homogeneity of variance assumption is satisfied. The ANOVA significance tests indicate main effects for both type of violence, $F(1, 28) = 35.80$, $p < .001$, partial $\eta^2 = .56$, and time of exposure, $F(1, 28) = 165.10$, $p < .001$, partial $\eta^2 = .86$, along with a significant interaction, $F(1,28) = 17.81$, $p < .001$, partial $\eta^2 = .39$ (see Figure 10-10). The profile plot (Figure 10-11) indicates that the kind of violence viewed affects subsequent aggressive behavior, and that the effect increases with time of exposure.

Descriptive Statistics

Dependent Variable:Aggressive Behavior

Type of Violence	Time of Exposure	Mean	Std. Deviation	N
Cartoon Violence	10 Minutes	49.13	3.720	8
	30 Minutes	66.25	4.166	8
	Total	57.69	9.631	16
Real Violence	10 Minutes	52.63	8.141	8
	30 Minutes	86.50	5.345	8
	Total	69.56	18.715	16
Total	10 Minutes	50.88	6.376	16
	30 Minutes	76.37	11.436	16
	Total	63.62	15.835	32

Levene's Test of Equality of Error Variances[a]

Dependent Variable:Aggressive Behavior

F	df1	df2	Sig.
2.193	3	28	.111

Tests the null hypothesis that the error variance of the dependent variable is equal across groups.

a. Design: Intercept + Type + Time + Type * Time

Figure 10-9 Descriptive statistics and homogeneity test

Tests of Between-Subjects Effects

Dependent Variable:Aggressive Behavior

Source	Type III Sum of Squares	df	Mean Square	F	Sig.	Partial Eta Squared
Corrected Model	6891.250[a]	3	2297.083	72.903	.000	.887
Intercept	129540.500	1	129540.500	4111.232	.000	.993
Type	1128.125	1	1128.125	35.803	.000	.561
Time	5202.000	1	5202.000	165.096	.000	.855
Type * Time	561.125	1	561.125	17.808	.000	.389
Error	882.250	28	31.509			
Total	137314.000	32				
Corrected Total	7773.500	31				

a. R Squared = .887 (Adjusted R Squared = .874)

Figure 10-10. Significance tests

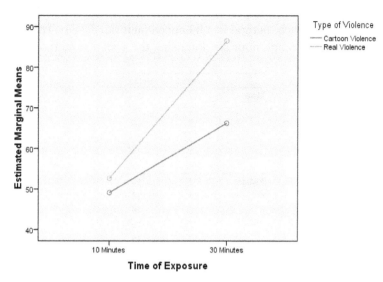

Figure 10-11. Profile plot of cell means

The interaction between time of exposure and type of violence observed is significant. Because this is an "ordinal" interaction (the lines do not cross), it is possible to examine main effects for the factors as well as the interaction effect. When interactions are "disordinal" in nature (the lines cross), main effects are difficult, if not impossible, to interpret.

More Complex ANOVA Designs

We have discussed one-way ANOVA, repeated-measures ANOVA, and two-way ANOVA with a balanced factorial design and two levels of each of two independent variables. SPSS is quite capable of handling more complex designs, including two-way ANOVA with three or more levels of an independent variable or variables. There are three-way or even more complex factorial designs and mixed models with one or more repeated measures and one or more between-groups factors. It is also possible to perform analysis of covariance (ANCOVA) with SPSS. Additionally, SPSS provides menus for multivariate analysis of variance (MANOVA) and covariance (MANCOVA). These designs are beyond our current scope. The reader should note that as the designs become more complex, the interpretation of effects and interactions becomes more complex as well, so there is little virtue to a design so complicated it is difficult to understand or explain to others.

Chapter 10 Exercises

1. A reading instructor interested in comparing the effects of two instructional methods randomly assigned male and female students to each method in a balanced factorial design. The data represent competency scores on a 20-item quiz after a one-hour session using the assigned method. Results are as follows:

	Method1	Method2
Male	19	17
	17	18
	15	16
	16	18
	17	15
	15	13
Female	10	15
	14	16
	13	18
	12	19
	14	19
	13	17

Build an appropriate SPSS data file. Conduct a two-way ANOVA with *Method* and *Sex* as fixed factors. Interpret the results.

2. Business researchers compared the productivity of retail outlets with introverted and extraverted leaders and passive and proactive team members. The data represent the retail outlet's profitability as a percentage of improvement over six weeks. The hypothetical data are as follows:

		Leader's Personality	
		Introverted	Extraverted
Team Members	Passive	0	12
		2	11
		-2	10
		3	7
		3	8
	Proactive	15	5
		18	9
		19	8
		20	4
		17	6

Build an appropriate SPSS data file. Conduct a two-way ANOVA with leader's personality and team personality as fixed factors. Interpret the results.

3. A medical research team compared two drugs for controlling blood glucose levels. Each drug was formulated as an extended release capsule and as an ordinary pill taken three times per day with meals. Patients with Type II diabetes were randomly assigned to four groups as shown below. The dependent variable is the patient's fasting blood glucose level after taking the medicine daily for ninety days.

	Drug1	Drug2
Ordinary	197	197
	266	145
	180	203
	252	125
	289	145
	303	194
Extended	211	180
	135	126
	157	235
	222	194
	186	199
	288	122

Build an appropriate SPSS data file. Conduct a two-way ANOVA with drug and pill type as fixed factors. Interpret the results.

11 Correlation and Regression

Objectives

1. Calculate correlation coefficients and test their significance.
2. Derive a linear regression equation.
3. Calculate and examine residuals.

Overview

Unlike experimental designs, designs using correlational research examine variables in their "natural state," without direct manipulation. The Pearson product-moment correlation coefficient is an index of the linear association between a predictor (independent variable) and a criterion (dependent variable). The coefficient ranges from −1 representing a perfect inverse or negative correlation through zero representing no relationship or complete independence to +1 representing a perfect positive or direct relationship between the predictor and the criterion. The square of the correlation coefficient is called the "coefficient of determination," and this value can be interpreted directly as a measure of the strength of the linear relationship between the predictor and the criterion.

Closely related to correlation is the topic of linear regression. If the correlation between two variables is significantly different from zero, a line can be used to model this relationship. The equation for this line of best fit includes an intercept term and a regression (slope) coefficient.

SPSS can easily calculate and test bivariate correlations, as well as derive the regression line, test the significance of the intercept and slope term, and calculate predicted Y values and residuals. SPSS can also produce scatter diagrams to assist in interpreting the relationship between the independent and dependent variables. We will explore all these features of SPSS in this chapter.

Example Data

Pace (2008) collected information regarding the use of laptop computers in the college classroom by 63 undergraduate students. Data included a 12-item scale that assessed the attitudes of the students toward laptop computers, the student's sex, the student's GPA, and the frequency of use of laptop computers during class for class-related and non-class-related activities. The data, available from the companion site as Chapter_11.sav, are as follows (see Table 11-1).

Table 11-1. *Student attitudes toward laptop computers*

ID	Attitude	Sex	GPA	ClassRel	NonRel	ID	Attitude	Sex	GPA	ClassRel	NonRel
1	39	1	2.60	2	5	33	51	1	2.00	5	3
2	43	1	3.70	2	2	34	33	0	3.85	3	1
3	28	0	3.64	2	4	35	41	0	2.38	3	5
4	52	1	3.00	5	3	36	23	0	3.56	2	2
5	26	1	2.80	3	2	37	31	0	3.00	4	4
6	34	1	3.60	3	3	38	13	0	3.64	1	3
7	34	0	3.30	4	4	39	40	0	3.30	4	4
8	19	0	3.66	1	2	40	35	1	3.13	4	4
9	32	0	3.52	3	5	41	39	0	3.00	2	2
10	31	0	4.00	2	3	42	29	0	2.60	5	3
11	28	0	3.80	1	1	43	30	0	3.59	2	2
12	33	0	3.23	3	3	44	46	0	3.30	4	3
13	19	0	3.40	4	2	45	37	0	2.50	4	5
14	31	0	3.20	3	4	46	30	0	3.70	5	5
15	38	1	3.10	5	4	47	34	0	4.00	4	3
16	24	0	3.40	1	1	48	39	0	3.10	4	5
17	48	1	3.20	4	4	49	39	0	2.55	5	5
18	26	0	3.53	2	3	50	45	0	2.60	5	2
19	43	0	2.78	4	4	51	33	0	4.00	3	3
20	37	0	3.00	4	5	52	26	0	3.79	3	5
21	31	0	3.20	4	5	53	43	1	2.40	3	3
22	16	1	3.40	1	1	54	42	1	2.50	5	4
23	44	0	3.01	5	5	55	37	0	1.40	4	3
24	30	0	3.80	1	1	56	34	1	2.70	3	2
25	39	0	2.80	4	4	57	27	0	3.00	2	4
26	43	1	3.46	4	5	58	35	0	3.09	4	4
27	30	0	3.70	3	3	59	41	0	3.60	3	4
28	24	0	3.40	2	2	60	36	0	2.50	3	3
29	29	0	3.20	5	5	61	20	0	2.50	2	3
30	31	0	3.00	4	3	62	44	0	3.70	3	1
31	32	0	3.00	3	3	63	38	1	3.20	3	2
32	46	0	3.30	4	5						

The data appropriately entered in SPSS appear in Figure 11-1. In particular, it will be interesting to determine whether using a laptop computer in class correlates positively with GPA, and whether students with more positive attitudes toward laptops are more likely to use them.

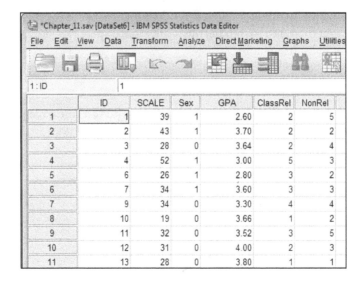

Figure 11-1. *Attitude data (partial data set)*

Calculating and Testing Correlations

To calculate and test the significance of bivariate correlations, use the **Analyze** menu in SPSS. Select **Analyze > Correlate > Bivariate** as shown in Figure 11-2. In the resulting dialog box, move the Attitude *SCALE*, *GPA*,

ClassRel, and *NonRel* to the Variables window (see Figure 11-3). Make sure the box in front of "Flag significant correlations" is checked. If you prefer, you can also click on **Options** and display means and standard deviations as well as other statistics. Click on **OK** to run the Correlations procedure. Figure 11-4 shows the resulting output.

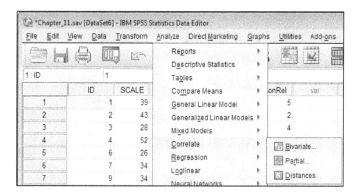

Figure 11-2. Select Analyze > Correlate > Bivariate

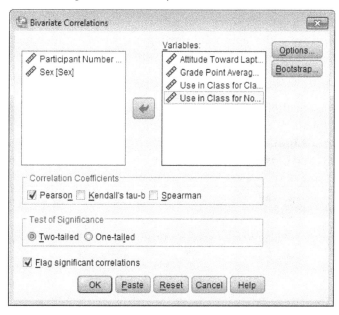

Figure 11-3. Bivariate Correlations dialog

Correlations

		Attitude Toward Laptops	Grade Point Average	Use in Class for Class Actitivites	Use in Class for Non-Class Activities
Attitude Toward Laptops	Pearson Correlation	1	-.352**	.587**	.303*
	Sig. (2-tailed)		.005	.000	.016
	N	63	63	63	63
Grade Point Average	Pearson Correlation	-.352**	1	-.412**	-.235
	Sig. (2-tailed)	.005		.001	.064
	N	63	63	63	63
Use in Class for Class Actitivites	Pearson Correlation	.587**	-.412**	1	.542**
	Sig. (2-tailed)	.000	.001		.000
	N	63	63	63	63
Use in Class for Non-Class Activities	Pearson Correlation	.303*	-.235	.542**	1
	Sig. (2-tailed)	.016	.064	.000	
	N	63	63	63	63

**. Correlation is significant at the 0.01 level (2-tailed).

*. Correlation is significant at the 0.05 level (2-tailed).

Figure 11-4. *Correlation output*

The student's GPA is significantly negatively correlated with the attitude toward laptop use, and attitudes predict both class-related and non-class use of the laptop. Interestingly, the class-related use of laptops correlates *negatively* with grades (Pace, 2008). Apparently, students were paying more attention to their computers than to their instructors.

Let us determine the regression equation for predicting the *SCALE* score from the class-related use of laptops. To find the values of the Y intercept and the regression coefficient, you would use the Regression procedure in SPSS. Select **Analyze > Regression> Linear** as shown in Figure 11-5. In the Linear Regression dialog, move *SCALE* to the dependent variable window and *ClassRel* to the Independent(s) window (see Figure 11-6).

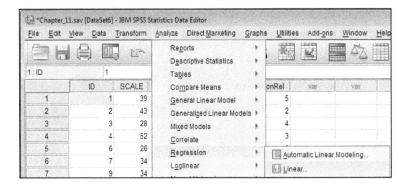

Figure 11-5. *Select Analyze > Regression > Linear*

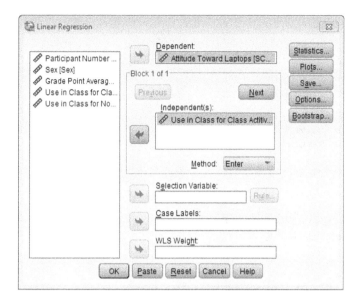

Figure 11-6. *Linear Regression Dialog*

You can enter more than one independent variable, and thus use the same tool for multiple regression, a topic beyond the scope of this basic text.

Click **OK** to run the Regression procedure. Figure 11-7 shows the output. The *Y*-intercept, labeled "Constant," is 20.875, and the unstandardized regression coefficient for predicting attitudes from in-class laptop use is 0.721. Note that in the bivariate case the standardized regression coefficient is equal to the Pearson *r* (see Figure 11-7).

Model Summary

Model	R	R Square	Adjusted R Square	Std. Error of the Estimate
1	.587ª	.344	.333	6.833

a. Predictors: (Constant), Use in Class for Class Actitivites

ANOVAb

Model		Sum of Squares	df	Mean Square	F	Sig.
1	Regression	1495.270	1	1495.270	32.022	.000ª
	Residual	2848.444	61	46.696		
	Total	4343.714	62			

a. Predictors: (Constant), Use in Class for Class Actitivites
b. Dependent Variable: Attitude Toward Laptops

Coefficientsa

Model		Unstandardized Coefficients		Standardized Coefficients		
		B	Std. Error	Beta	t	Sig.
1	(Constant)	20.875	2.498		8.357	.000
	Use in Class for Class Actitivites	4.077	.721	.587	5.659	.000

a. Dependent Variable: Attitude Toward Laptops

Figure 11-7. *Regression procedure output*

Scatterplots

Let us construct a scatterplot of the relationship between attitudes and class-related laptop use. Select **Graphs** > **Chart Builder**, and then select Scatter/Dot as the chart type. Click on the Simple Scatter diagram and then drag it into the Chart Builder window. Now drag *SCALE* to the *Y* axis and *ClassRel* to the *X* axis (see Figure 11-8).

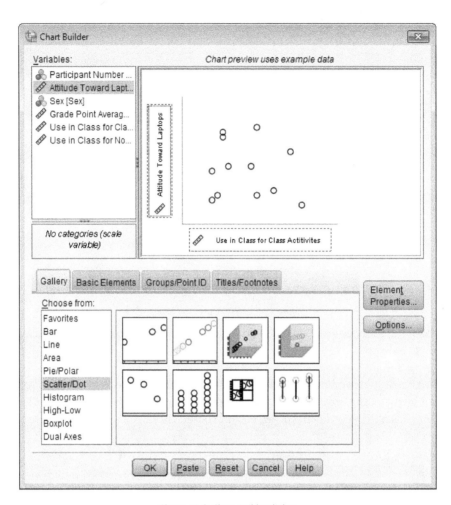

Figure 11-8. Chart Builder dialog

The chart preview uses example data. The actual scatterplot appears in the SPSS Viewer. Double-click on the chart object to open and edit it to add a fit line (see Figure 11-9).

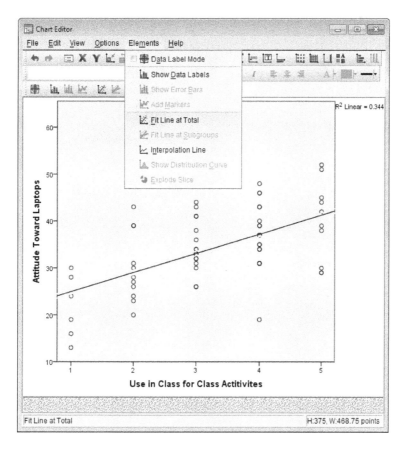

Figure 11-9. Scatterplot with fit line added

Calculating and Interpreting Residuals

SPSS can calculate and save either raw score or standardized predicted values and residuals. Let us use the same regression as before, the regression of *SCALE* on *ClassRel*. We will specify that SPSS should calculate raw-score predicted values and residuals. We will also examine plots of the residuals.

In the Linear Regression Dialog (refer to Figure 11-6), click on **Save** and then check the boxes in front of "Unstandardized" for Predicted Values and Residuals (see Figure 11-10).

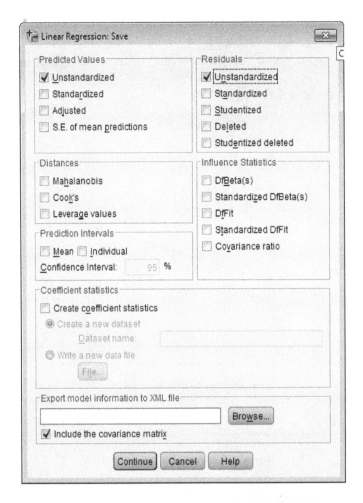

Figure 11-10. *Select unstandardized predicted values and residuals*

When you run the regression procedure, SPSS will calculate the predicted values of *Y* according to the regression equation and will subtract the predicted value from the observed value of *Y* for each observation. SPSS will save these values as new variables in the data file. You can also click on **Plots** to examine various residual plots. Two of the most instructive of these are the histogram of the standardized residuals and the normal probability plot (see Figure 11-11).

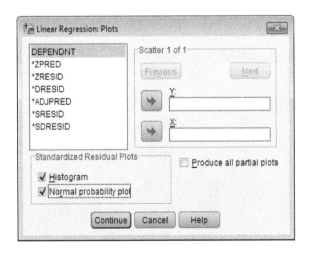

Figure 11-11. *Linear Regression: Plots dialog*

Click **Continue** then **OK** to run the regression. The predicted values and residuals appear as new variables (see Figure 11-12). The histogram of the standardized residuals (Figure 11-13) and the normal probability plot (Figure 11-14) appear in the SPSS viewer. The normal p-p plot of the standardized residuals displays the actual and expected cumulative probabilities of the residuals under the assumption that they are normally distributed. Of course, you could also do a test of normality to determine if the residuals meet that assumption, as you learned in Chapter 4.

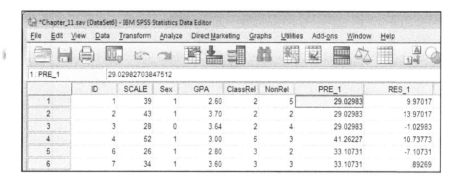

Figure 11-12. Predicted values and residuals are saved as new variables

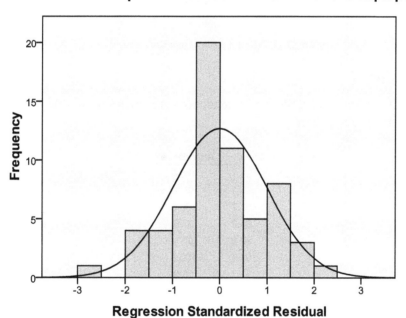

Figure 11-13. Histogram of standardized residuals

Dependent Variable: Attitude Toward Laptops

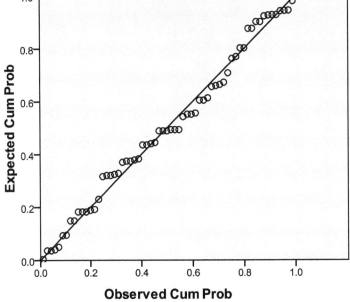

Figure 11-14. Normal p-p plot of standardized residuals

Chapter 11 Exercises

1. The following data are the final grades and attendance percentages of 19 college students in a statistics class (data collected by the author).

Grade	Attendance
95.7	100.0
85.3	95.1
92.7	100.0
85.2	97.6
80.6	95.1
91.4	100.0
82.7	82.9
86.5	100.0
83.0	85.4
82.0	95.1
94.9	100.0
75.7	92.7
86.3	100.0
89.5	100.0
91.5	100.0
87.0	97.6
85.2	100.0
88.3	95.1
85.2	90.2

Build an appropriate SPSS data file. Calculate the correlation between grades and attendance and test the significance of the correlation. Determine the percentage of variation in grades that can be explained by knowing the student's attendance percentage.

2. Using the data from exercise 1 above, perform a regression analysis. What is the linear regression equation? Display a histogram and a normal probability plot of the residuals.

3. Two supervisors independently rated the productivity of eight workers on a 10-point scale, with 10 representing the highest productivity. We assume the scale is interval in nature. The hypothetical data are as follows.

Worker	Rater1	Rater2
1	4	4
2	2	2
3	4	2
4	1	2
5	7	5
6	5	6
7	6	7
8	8	8

Build an appropriate SPSS data file. Find the correlation between the ratings of the two supervisors, and test the correlation for significance.

4. Using the data from exercise 1 above, perform a regression analysis treating the rating of Rater 2 as the dependent variable. What is the linear regression equation? Display a histogram and a normal probability plot of the residuals.

12 Chi-Square Tests

Objectives

1. Perform and interpret chi-square tests of goodness-of-fit.
2. Perform and interpret chi-square tests of independence.
3. Examine effect size for tests of independence.

Overview

Many behavioral science data are categorical in nature, and the only mathematical operation applicable to such data is to count the numbers in the categories. It is still useful, however, to compare such counts of observed frequencies to what you would expect under a null hypothesis.

Chi-square (χ^2) tests are be used to determine whether the observed frequencies in the categories of a single nominal variable deviate significantly from expectation. These are goodness-of-fit tests. Chi-square tests can also be used to determine whether the observed and expected frequencies in a two-way classification table differ significantly. These tests are chi-square tests of independence. In this chapter you will learn both chi-square tests. We will use the Nonparametric Tests menu in SPSS for the goodness-of-fit test and the Crosstabs procedure for the test of independence.

Example Data

Assume that you are interested in the effects of peer mentoring on grades and student retention at a private liberal arts college. You randomly select a group of 30 students during their freshman orientation. These students are assigned to a team of seniors who have been trained as tutors in various academic subjects, listening skills, and team-building skills. The selected students meet in small group sessions with their mentors once each week during their entire freshman year, are encouraged to work with their small group for study sessions, and are encouraged to schedule private sessions with their peer mentors whenever they desire. You identify an additional 30 students at orientation as a control group. The control group members receive no formal peer mentoring. You determine that there are no significant differences between the high school grades and SAT scores of the two groups. At the end of four years, you compare the two groups on retention and grades. The example data appear in Table 12-1.

Table 12-1. Hypothetical peer mentoring data

Participant	Mentored	Grades	Retention	Participant	Mentored	Grades	Retention
1	1	1	2	31	0	0	0
2	1	1	2	32	0	1	1
3	1	1	2	33	0	1	1
4	1	1	1	34	0	0	0
5	1	1	2	35	0	0	1
6	1	1	2	36	0	1	1
7	1	1	2	37	0	0	0
8	1	1	1	38	0	1	1
9	1	0	1	39	0	0	0
10	1	0	2	40	0	0	1
11	1	1	1	41	0	0	0
12	1	0	1	42	0	1	1
13	1	0	2	43	0	1	1
14	1	1	0	44	0	0	2
15	1	0	2	45	0	1	0
16	1	0	1	46	0	0	0
17	1	0	2	47	0	1	0
18	1	0	0	48	0	0	1
19	1	1	2	49	0	0	1
20	1	1	2	50	0	1	2
21	1	0	2	51	0	1	2
22	1	1	1	52	0	1	1
23	1	1	2	53	0	1	2
24	1	0	2	54	0	0	1
25	1	1	1	55	0	1	1
26	1	0	2	56	0	1	1
27	1	1	1	57	0	1	1
28	1	1	2	58	0	0	1
29	1	1	2	59	0	1	0
30	1	1	2	60	0	1	2

You code *Mentored* as 1 (*present*) and 0 (*absent*) to identify the two groups. Because GPAs differ by academic major, you generate a binary code for *Grades*. If the student's cumulative GPA is at the median or higher for his or her academic major, you assign a 1. Students whose grades are below the median for their major receive a 0. If the student is no longer enrolled (i.e., has transferred, dropped out, or flunked out), you code a 0 for *Retention*. If he or she is still enrolled, but has not yet graduated after four years, you code a 1. If he or she has graduated, you code a 2. Properly entered in SPSS, the data should have the structure shown in Figure 12-1. These data are available on the companion web page.

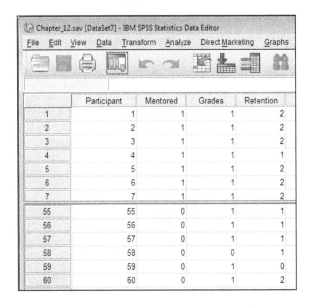

Figure 12-1. Peer monitoring data in SPSS (partial data)

Conducting a Goodness-of-Fit Test

You can perform a goodness-of-fit test to determine whether the three retention outcomes are equally distributed. Because there are three possible outcomes (no longer enrolled, currently enrolled, and graduated) and sixty total students, you would expect each outcome to be observed in one-third of the cases if there were no differences in the frequencies of these outcomes. The null hypothesis would be that 20 students would not be enrolled, 20 would be currently enrolled, and 20 would have graduated after four years. To test this hypothesis, you use the Nonparametric Tests procedure. Select **Analyze** > **Nonparametric Tests** > **Legacy Dialogs** > **Chi-Square** as shown in Figure 12-2.

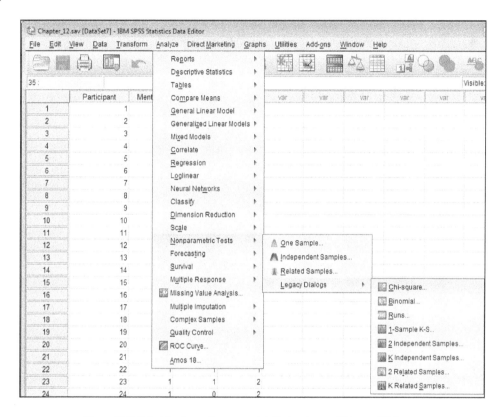

Figure 12-2. Select Analyze > Nonparametric Tests > Legacy Dialogs > Chi-Square

In the resulting dialog box, move *Retention* into the Test Variable List and accept the default for equal expected frequencies (All categories equal). See Figure 12-3. Click **OK** to run the chi-square test.

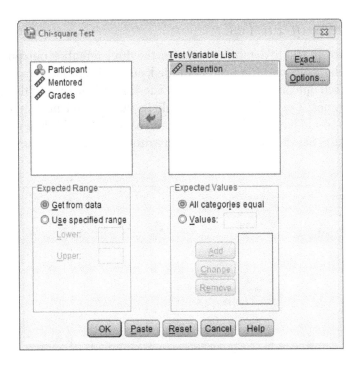

Figure 12-3. *Chi-Square Test dialog*

SPSS counts and tabulates the observed frequencies and performs the chi-square test (see the SPSS Viewer output in Figure 12-4). The degrees of freedom for the goodness-of-fit test are the number of categories minus one. The significant chi-square shows that the frequencies are not equally distributed, χ^2 (2, N = 60) = 6.10, p = .047.

Chi-Square Test

Frequencies

Retention

	Observed N	Expected N	Residual
Not Enrolled	11	20.0	-9.0
Enrolled	25	20.0	5.0
Graduated	24	20.0	4.0
Total	60		

Test Statistics

	Retention
Chi-Square	6.100[a]
df	2
Asymp. Sig.	.047

a. 0 cells (.0%) have expected frequencies less than 5. The minimum expected cell frequency is 20.0.

Figure 12-4. *Goodness-of-fit test output*

When the null hypothesis states that the expected frequencies are not equal, you can specify the expected values by clicking on the radio button in front of "Values" in the Chi-Square Test dialog (see Figure 12-3).

Conducting a Chi-Square Test of Independence

If mentoring and retention are not related, you would expect mentored and non-mentored students to have the same outcomes, so that any observed differences in frequencies would be due to chance. You would expect half of the students in each outcome group to come from the mentored students, and the other half to come from the non-mentored students. To test the hypothesis that there is an association (or non-independence) between mentoring and retention, we will conduct a chi-square test as part of the cross-tabulation procedure. To conduct the test, select **Analyze** > **Descriptive Statistics** > **Crosstabs** (see Figure 12-5).

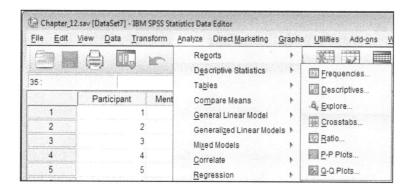

Figure 12-5. Select Analyze > Descriptive Statistics > Crosstabs

In the Crosstabs dialog, move one variable to the Row(s) field and the other variable to the Column(s) field. You can place the variable with more levels in the row field to keep the output tables narrower (see Figure 12-6), though the results of the test would be identical if you reverse the row and column variables. Request clustered bar charts (see Figure 12-6) for a visual examination of the categories. In the **Statistics** dialog, select "Chi-square" and "Phi and Cramér's *V*," which are measures of effect size for chi-square. See Figure 12-7. Select **Continue** to return to the Crosstabs dialog. Click on "Display clustered bar charts." You can also click on **Cells** to display both expected and observed frequencies. After returning to the Crosstabs dialog, click **OK** to run the cross-tabulation and chi-square test.

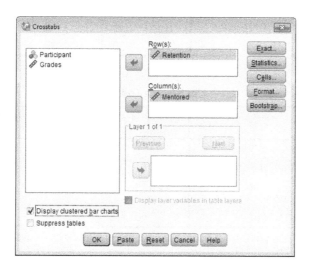

Figure 12-6. Crosstabs dialog

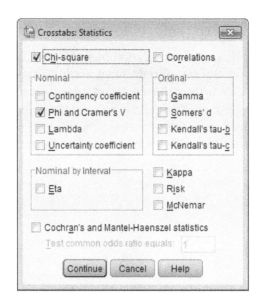

Figure 12-7. Crosstabs Statistics dialog

The SPSS Viewer output in Figure 12-8 shows the results of the cross-tabulation and chi-square test. The Pearson Chi-Square is significant, indicating that mentoring had an effect on retention, χ^2 (2, N = 60) = 14.58, p < .001. The value of Cramér's V is .493, indicating a large effect size. The clustered bar charts (see Figure 12-9) clearly show the effect of mentoring on retention.

Retention * Mentored Crosstabulation

Count

		Mentored		Total
		Not Mentored	Mentored	
Retention	Not Enrolled	9	2	11
	Enrolled	16	9	25
	Graduated	5	19	24
Total		30	30	60

Chi-Square Tests

	Value	df	Asymp. Sig. (2-sided)
Pearson Chi-Square	14.581[a]	2	.001
Likelihood Ratio	15.512	2	.000
Linear-by-Linear Association	13.474	1	.000
N of Valid Cases	60		

a. 0 cells (.0%) have expected count less than 5. The minimum expected count is 5.50.

Figure 12-8. Cross-tabulation and chi-square test results

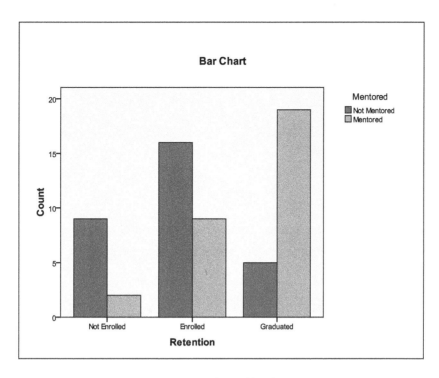

Figure 12-9. Clustered bar chart

Chi-Square Test of Independence with Summary Data

We sometimes encounter frequency data that are in a contingency table rather than in raw data format. For example, consider the following data concerning the use of various computational tools by professors who teach statistics in different departments.

Table 12-2. Computational tools used in statistics classes

Department	SPSS	Excel	Minitab	Total
Psychology	21	6	4	31
Business	6	19	8	33
Mathematics	5	7	12	24
Total	32	32	24	88

We can enter these data as nine rows in an SPSS data file and weight the cases by the frequencies. Let us use the numbers 1 – 3 to represent the department, and use the same numbers to represent the computational tools. Here is how the data should look (Figure 12-10):

	Department	Tool	Frequency
1	1	1	21
2	1	2	6
3	1	3	4
4	2	1	6
5	2	2	19
6	2	3	8
7	3	1	5
8	3	2	7
9	3	3	12

Figure 12-10. Contingency table entered in SPSS

To weight the cases by frequency, select **Data** > **Weight Cases**, and move Frequency into the "Weight cases by" field (Figure 12-11). Click **OK**.

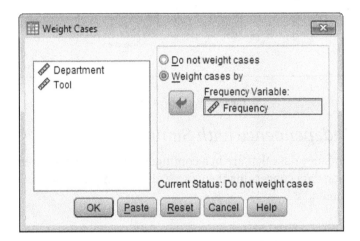

Figure 12-11. Weight Cases dialog box

Now, run the Crosstabs procedure as described above, using *Tool* as the column variable and *Department* as the row variable. The output shows the application of the frequency weighting to produce the same contingency table shown in Table 12-2, and the results indicate a significant association between the department and the computational tool (Figure 12-12).

Case Processing Summary

	Cases					
	Valid		Missing		Total	
	N	Percent	N	Percent	N	Percent
Department * Tool	88	100.0%	0	.0%	88	100.0%

Department * Tool Crosstabulation

Count

		Tool			Total
		SPSS	Excel	Mintab	
Department	Psychology	21	6	4	31
	Business	6	19	8	33
	Mathematics	5	7	12	24
Total		32	32	24	88

Chi-Square Tests

	Value	df	Asymp. Sig. (2-sided)
Pearson Chi-Square	26.881[a]	4	.000
Likelihood Ratio	25.724	4	.000
Linear-by-Linear Association	15.781	1	.000
N of Valid Cases	88		

a. 0 cells (.0%) have expected count less than 5. The minimum expected count is 6.55.

Figure 12-12. Chi-square test from summary data

It is also possible to use the summary approach with frequency weighting for a chi-square test of goodness of fit. In this case, the user can enter observed frequencies and weight cases by these observed frequencies. Select **Analyze > Nonparametric Tests > Legacy Dialogs > Chi-square**. If the expected values are all equal, keep the default "All categories equal" under "Expected Values." If the expected values are not equal, click the radio button in front of "Values," and enter the expected values one at a time, clicking **Add** after each entry.

Chapter 12 Exercises

1. A dietitian randomly selected a total of 100 cereal boxes from the bottom, middle, and top shelves of a local grocery store. The dietitian rated the nutritional value of each cereal as low, medium, or high, based on fiber, vitamins, calories, sodium, and sugar content. These are the data:

Shelf	Nutritional Value			Total
	Low	Medium	High	
Bottom	27	15	5	47
Middle	10	12	7	29
Top	5	5	14	24
Total	42	32	26	100

Presumably, children more easily see the cereal boxes on the lower shelves, and adults more easily see the cereal boxes on the higher shelves. Does there appear to be an association between the location of the cereal and the nutritional value? Perform a chi-square test of independence using the frequency weighting method described in this chapter. Use numerical codes for position and nutritional value.

2. The following data were collected by the members of a statistics class, who opened 7 small bags of Plain
    M&Ms and 8 small bags of Peanut M&Ms and counted the frequencies of each color. Using the frequency
    weighting method described in this chapter, perform a chi-square test of independence to determine
    whether the type of candy is associated with the color distribution. Use numerical codes for the colors and
    the types (plain or peanut).

	Type		
Color	Plain	Peanut	Total
Blue	78	40	118
Red	47	26	73
Yellow	46	19	65
Green	56	28	84
Orange	98	37	135
Brown	68	22	90
Total	393	172	565

3. Forty-two students who liked M&Ms and expressed a color preference provided the following data
    concerning their favorite colors. Using the weighting strategy discussed above, test the hypothesis that the
    preferences are equally distributed. Note the expected frequency for each color if the null hypothesis is
    true is 7. You should use a numeric code to represent the colors and use that variable as the test variable.

Color	Preference
Blue	13
Green	11
Red	8
Brown	5
Yellow	3
Orange	2
Total	42

13 Nonparametric Tests

Objectives

1. Recognize when to use nonparametric tests.
2. Perform and interpret nonparametric tests for paired samples.
3. Perform and interpret nonparametric tests for two independent samples.
4. Perform and interpret nonparametric tests for three or more independent groups.

Overview

The *t* tests and ANOVAs you learned in previous chapters are *parametric* tests because they make estimates or inferences about population parameters, and because they make assumptions about the distributional characteristics of the population from which the sample is drawn. Nonparametric tests make few or no distributional assumptions, and usually do not estimate population parameters.

There are two primary occasions when you might choose a nonparametric test rather than a parametric one. In one case you have little choice in the matter because of the nature of the data you have collected. Nonparametric tests are always appropriate when your data are ordinal rather than scale measures (interval or ratio). In the second case, you may choose to use a nonparametric test when your data violate the assumptions for a parametric test—for example when the data are markedly non-normal or when the data fail to meet the assumption of homogeneity of variance.

Nonparametric tests are generally (though not always) less powerful than parametric tests, and in some cases, simple transformations of the raw data such as square root or logarithmic transformations may allow you to use parametric procedures rather than nonparametric ones. Such transformations are easy to do using the Transform menu in SPSS.

In this chapter you will learn nonparametric alternatives for paired-samples data, two independent samples, and three or more independent samples. The tests we discuss tend to be among the more powerful and useful of the nonparametric procedures. The particular tests we examine use ranks—either because the data were ranks originally, or because we convert the data to ranks.

The Wilcoxon Matched-Pairs Signed-Ranks Test

The Wilcoxon matched-pairs signed-ranks test is a nonparametric alternative to the paired-samples *t* test. Calculate the difference between the two scores for each pair, and then rank these differences from 1 to N according to the magnitude of the difference (ignoring sign). Next, sum separately the absolute values of the ranks associated with positive differences and negative differences. The smaller of these two sums is T, the test statistic. There is the possibility of tied values for the members of a given pair, in which case the conservative treatment is to discard the scores for that pair and reduce N by 1.

Tables of the critical values of the T statistic are readily available for small sample sizes, but with larger samples the value of T is approximately normally distributed. Regardless of sample size, SPSS uses the normal approximation and reports z for the significance test.

Example Data

A psychology professor has developed an individualized program of instruction in critical thinking that he believes will improve the quiz scores of his introductory psychology students. He chooses a random sample of eight students and measures their grades on two equivalent forms of a chapter quiz before and after the instructional program. To control for order effects, half the students received Form A first and the other half of the students receiving Form B first. The results are as follows. The data are available as Chapter_13A.sav.

Table 13-1. Hypothetical Quiz Scores

Student	Before	After
1	57	65
2	60	64
3	66	70
4	69	82
5	74	94
6	87	87
7	90	97
8	10	97

Performing the Test

Enter and structure the data in SPSS as you have previously learned. As with the paired-samples *t* test, enter the two measures for each case in separate columns. Select **Analyze > Nonparametric Tests >Legacy Dialogs > 2 Related Samples** (see Figure 13-1). In the dialog box, indicate the pairing of *Before* and *After* scores for each student and select the Wilcoxon test (see Figure 13-2).

The SPSS Viewer output shows that the Wilcoxon Signed-Ranks Test results are significant. Quiz scores are significantly higher after the instruction in critical thinking. See Figure 13-3. In six of the eight cases, the *After* measure was higher than the *Before* measure. One case was tied, and in one case the *After* measure was lower than the *Before* measure.

You can also use another nonparametric test called the "sign" test in this situation, but instead of the sums of the absolute values of ranks, it uses only information regarding the direction of the difference between the two scores. The sign test is therefore generally less powerful than the Wilcoxon test.

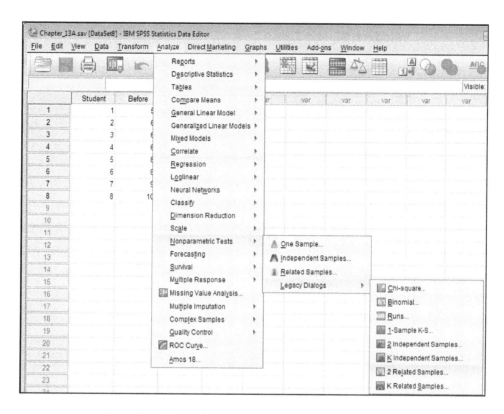

Figure 13-1. *Select Analyze > Nonparametric Tests > 2 Related Samples*

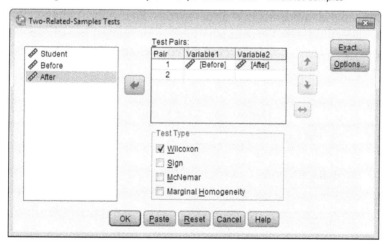

Figure 13-2. *Two-Related Samples Tests dialog*

Wilcoxon Signed Ranks Test

Ranks

		N	Mean Rank	Sum of Ranks
After - Before	Negative Ranks	1 [a]	1.50	1.50
	Positive Ranks	6 [b]	4.42	26.50
	Ties	1 [c]		
	Total	8		

a. After < Before
b. After > Before
c. After = Before

Test Statistics[b]

	After - Before
Z	-2.120 [a]
Asymp. Sig. (2-tailed)	.034

a. Based on negative ranks.
b. Wilcoxon Signed Ranks Test

Figure 13-3. Wilcoxon Matched-Pairs Signed-Ranks Test results

Our hypothesis test revealed that the after scores are significantly higher than the before scores, $z = -2.12$, $p = .034$.

Note that you can achieve the same result using **Analyze > Nonparametric Tests > Related Samples**. Enter *Before* and *After* as the test fields, and click the Run button. SPSS chooses the "Related-Samples Wilcoxon Signed Rank Test," and reports the same significance level as before (see Figure 13-4), though the actual test statistic is not reported. However, double-clicking on the summary table in the output launches a "Model Viewer" window with significant detail, including a chart of the observed differences and the test statistics. You can click on Edit to copy the auxiliary view (see Figure 13-5).

Hypothesis Test Summary

	Null Hypothesis	Test	Sig.	Decision
1	The median of differences between Before and After equals 0.	Related-Samples Wilcoxon Signed Rank Test	.034	Reject the null hypothesis.

Asymptotic significances are displayed. The significance level is .05.

Figure 13-4. Using Analyze > Nonparametric Tests > Related Samples

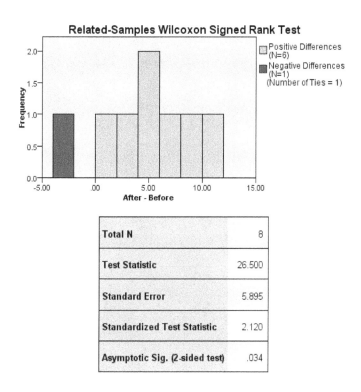

Total N	8
Test Statistic	26.500
Standard Error	5.895
Standardized Test Statistic	2.120
Asymptotic Sig. (2-sided test)	.034

Figure 13-5. SPSS 20 Model Viewer (Auxiliary window)

The Mann-Whitney U Test

The Mann-Whitney U Test provides a nonparametric alternative to the independent-samples t test. This test makes no assumption of normality of distribution, and compares the ranks for the two groups on a dependent variable either collected initially as ranks or converted to ranks. The test statistic U is based on the number of times a rank from one group is preceded by a rank from the other group. If there were no overlap at all, the ranks for the two groups would be completely separate, and the value of U would be zero. This would indicate that you could use group membership to predict the summed ranks for each group with perfect accuracy.

This test is best suited for small samples sizes where each group contains 20 or fewer observations. The groups need not have equal numbers of observations. Rank the scores from lowest to highest for the entire data set. One handles tied ranks in the usual manner of assigning the average rank of the two or more observations with the same score to each observation. The ranks for the observations in each of the two groups are summed, and U is derived from these summed ranks. Tabled values of U are available for small sample sizes, and for larger samples, the normal distribution provides a good approximation.

Example Data

The following fictitious data (see Table 13-2) show comparisons for 10 males and 10 females on a "Safe Driving Index," which is ordinal in nature at best. Higher scores indicate safer driving practices. The data are available as Chapter_13B.sav.

Table 13-2 Example data for Mann-Whitney test

Male	Female
10	12
10	13
12	15
13	16
13	17
14	18
14	19
15	19
16	19
20	20

Performing the Test

As with the independent samples *t* test, you should enter the data in a single column in SPSS with a grouping variable to indicate the participant's sex (see Figure 13-6). To perform the Mann-Whitney test, select **Analyze** > **Nonparametric Tests** > **Legacy Dialogs** > **2 Independent Samples** (see Figure 13-7).

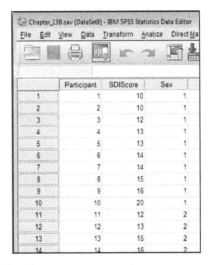

Figure 13-6. Data for Mann-Whitney test in SPSS (partial data)

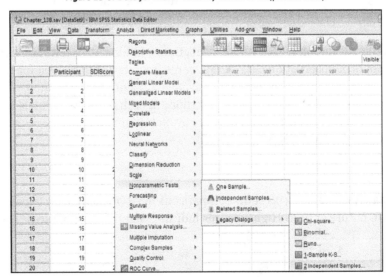

Figure 13-7. Select Analyze > Nonparametric Tests > 2 Independent Samples

In the dialog, enter the dependent variable *SDIScore* in the Test Variable List and *Sex* as the Grouping Variable (see Figure 13-8). You will need to click on the **Define Groups** button to specify the group codes as you did with the independent-samples *t* test. Select **Continue**, and then click **OK** to run the test. Figure 13-9 shows the Mann-Whitney test results from the SPSS Viewer. The mean rank for women is significantly higher than the mean rank for men, indicating at least in this study that women are safer drivers than men, $z = -2.05$, $p = .04$.

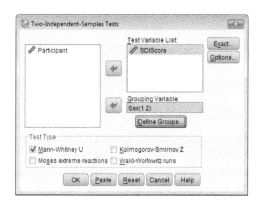

Figure 13-8. *Two-Independent-Samples Tests dialog*

Mann-Whitney Test

Ranks

	Sex	N	Mean Rank	Sum of Ranks
SDIScore	Male	10	7.80	78.00
	Female	10	13.20	132.00
	Total	20		

Test Statistics[b]

	SDIScore
Mann-Whitney U	23.000
Wilcoxon W	78.000
Z	-2.052
Asymp. Sig. (2-tailed)	.040
Exact Sig. [2*(1-tailed Sig.)]	.043[a]

a. Not corrected for ties.

b. Grouping Variable: Sex

Figure 13-9. *Mann-Whitney U Test results*

You can also achieve the same result by selecting **Analyze > Nonparametric Tests > Independent Samples**. Accept the default objective, and click on **Fields** to move *SDIScore* to the Test Fields window and *Sex* to the Groups field. Click on **Run** to conduct the test. As before, SPSS chooses the same test and reports the same *p* value. You can double-click on the "Hypothesis Test Summary" table to see the SPSS Model Viewer (not shown).

The Kruskal-Wallis Test

The Kruskal-Wallis "Analysis of Variance" for ranked data is a nonparametric alternative to the one-way ANOVA. You can think of the Kruskal-Wallis test as a direct extension of the Mann-Whitney *U* Test to three or more groups. Collapse the data across groups and rank the scores from lowest to highest. Then sum the ranks associated with each group separately. As with the Mann-Whitney test, there is no requirement that the groups have equal numbers of observations. The Kruskal-Wallis test produces a test statistic, *H*, which is approximately distributed as chi-square.

Example Data

The following hypothetical data represent performance of randomly assigned groups on a problem-solving task. Each group learns a different technique for solving the task (See Table 13-3). The dependent variable is a task-performance score. The data are available as Chapter_13C.sav.

Table 13-3. Hypothetical problem solving data

Group1	Group2	Group3
26	17	30
23	15	25
19	14	20
17	12	18
15	10	16

Enter the data exactly as you would for a one-way ANOVA, with a column for the dependent variable and a column for the grouping variable (see Figure 13-8). A test of homogeneity of variance indicates that the three group variances are significantly different. You will recall that this test is available as an option in the **Analyze > Compare Means> One-Way ANOVA** Options dialog. Because our data fail to meet the assumption of homoscedasticity, we will perform the Kruskal-Wallis Test as a nonparametric alternative to the ANOVA.

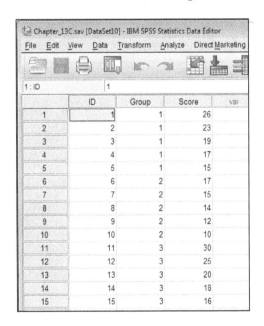

Figure 13-10. Data for Kruskal-Wallis test in SPSS

Performing the Test

To perform the Kruskal-Wallis test, select **Analyze > Nonparametric Tests > Legacy Dialogs > K Independent Samples** (see Figure 13-11).

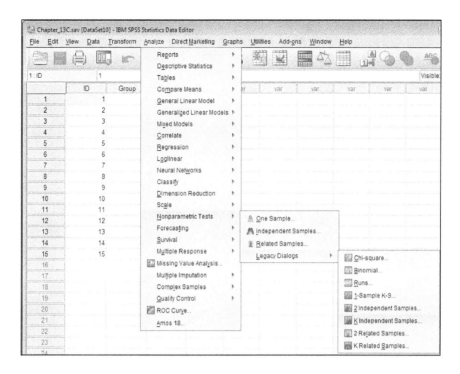

Figure 13-11. *Select Analyze > Nonparametric Tests > Legacy Dialogs > K Independent Samples*

In the dialog, enter *Score* as the Test Variable and *Group* as the Grouping Variable (see Figure 13-12). Make sure that the box in front of Kruskal-Wallis is checked. Click on **Define Range** to specify the levels of the grouping variable (from 1 to 3) and then click **Continue** and **OK** to run the Kruskal-Wallis test. The results of the Kruskal-Wallis test appear in the SPSS Viewer (Figure 13-13). The results indicate that the three training methods produce different levels of performance on the problem-solving task, χ^2 (2, N = 15) = 7.47, p = .024.

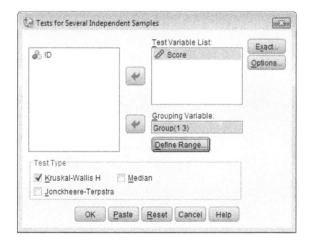

Figure 13-12. *Tests for Several Independent Samples dialog*

With multiple groups, a significant value of H (or chi-square) indicates an overall difference in the shapes of the distributions for the groups, but does not locate the groups that differ significantly from one another. Common practice is to use the Mann-Whitney U test as a post hoc comparison procedure after a significant overall Kruskal-Wallis test. The researcher can use "Bonferroni-corrected" alpha levels to ensure that these comparisons do not compound Type I error. In the current case, if the overall alpha level was .05, because there are three groups the significance level for each post hoc comparison should be held to .0167.

Kruskal-Wallis Test

Ranks

	Group	N	Mean Rank
Score	1	5	9.60
	2	5	3.60
	3	5	10.80
	Total	15	

Test Statistics[a,b]

	Score
Chi-Square	7.467
df	2
Asymp. Sig.	.024

a. Kruskal Wallis Test

b. Grouping Variable: Group

Figure 13-13. Kruskal-Wallis Test results

As in the previous two examples, you can run this same test using **Analyze** > **Nonparametric Tests** > **Independent Samples**. Accept the default objective, enter Score as the test field, and Group as the grouping variable. Click on Run to produce the Hypothesis Testing Summary table, which also provides access to the SPSS Model Viewer. As in the previous two cases, SPSS chooses the same test we did and produces the same p value. SPSS produced side-by-side boxplots (see figure 13-4). As an additional bonus, one does not have to specify the levels of the grouping variable.

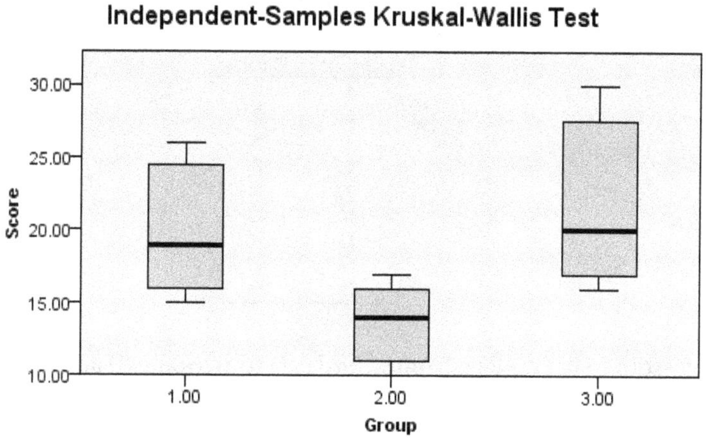

Independent-Samples Kruskal-Wallis Test

Total N	15
Test Statistic	7.467
Degrees of Freedom	2
Asymptotic Sig. (2-sided test)	.024

1. The test statistic is adjusted for ties.

Figure 13-14. SPSS Model Viewer auxiliary window

Chapter 13 Exercises

1. The following data represent measures on an Attitudes Toward Statistics scale before and after a statistics course. Higher numbers indicate more positive attitudes. Build an appropriate SPSS file. Perform and interpret a Wilcoxon matched-pairs signed-ranks test.

Before	After
50	48
40	50
55	60
48	53
42	51
45	49
51	78
55	62
62	57

Build an appropriate SPSS file. Conduct a Kruskal-Wallis test and interpret the results.

2. The following hypothetical ordinal data represent two independent groups of observations. Build an appropriate SPSS file. Perform and interpret a Mann-Whitney U test.

Group1	Group2
1	2
3	5
4	8
6	9
7	11
10	12
13	16
14	17
15	18

3. A dean ranked professors in her college from 1 (*highest*) to 15 (*lowest*) according to student ratings of teaching effectiveness. The dean then separated the professors into three groups (*low, medium,* and *high*) based on research productivity and service. Build an appropriate SPSS data file. Use a Kruskal-Wallis test to determine whether the teaching effectiveness rankings of the three groups of professors are equal.

Low	Medium	High
7	2	1
11	5	3
13	9	4
14	10	6
15	12	8

14 Data Handling

Objectives

1. Select records.
2. Sort records.
3. Split a file.
4. Recode variables.
5. Restructure data.

Overview

In Chapter 2, you learned how to establish an effective data structure by entering data and labeling the variables and values. You also learned to compute a new variable using the Transform menu and to delete records and variables. In this optional chapter, you will learn a few more techniques for manipulating data including selecting and sorting data records, splitting a file, and recoding a variable into the same or a different variable.

Selecting Records

You can choose selected cases from the **Data** > **Select Cases** menu. The cases you do not select are filtered or optionally deleted from the data file. When you select cases, only the selected cases are included in further analyses until you select the remaining cases again.

Let us revisit the data from Chapter 2 and select the cases for females only. Our criterion will be the *Sex* variable. Because female is coded as 1, we will select only cases for which the *Sex* value is 1. We will filter, but not delete, the cases for males. When cases are filtered, a diagonal line will appear in the row number area to indicate the exclusion of those records. To select the records for females, enter **Data** > **Select Cases** as shown in Figure 14-1.

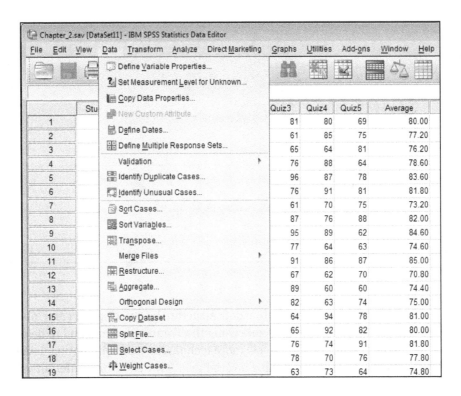

Figure 14-1. *Click Data > Select Cases*

In the dialog, click the radio button in front of "If condition is satisfied" (see Figure 14-2) and then click the button labeled "**If...**"

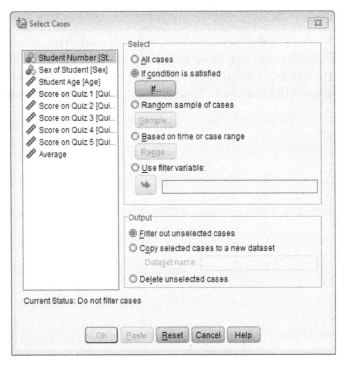

Figure 14-2. *The Select Cases dialog*

When you click the **If...** button, a new window allows you to enter the selection condition (see Figure 14-3). Enter Sex = 1 in the blank window. As with the Transform menu, you can point and click to enter variable names and operators, or type the condition directly. When you are finished, select **Continue** and then click **OK**. When you examine the Data View, you will see that the records for male students are now filtered and will be excluded from any further analyses until they are selected again. The records for males have a diagonal line through the row number field (see Figure 14-4).

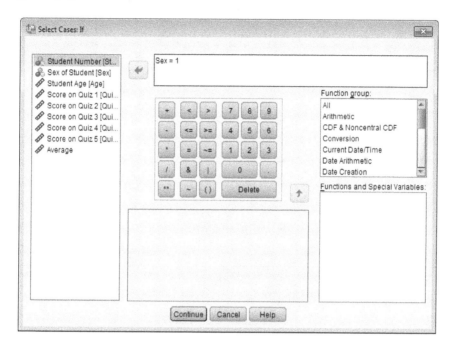

Figure 14-3. Select Cases condition dialog

Using the **Descriptive Statistics** > **Descriptives** command to summarize the ages indicates the records for females only are included (see Figure 14-5). When you examine both the Data View and the Variable View, you see that SPSS has created a new variable. It is named Filter_$, and corresponds to the filter criterion, Sex = 1. If you decide later to select records based on *Sex* again, you can use this filter variable rather than recreating the condition. To use this filter variable, click on the radio button in front of "Use filter variable" in the Select Cases dialog (see Figure 14-2) and then enter the filter variable in the active field.

You can reselect the records for males by returning to the Data menu and clicking on the radio button in front of "Select all cases" (see Figure 14-2). Let us do that so that we can sort all the cases by *Sex* and *Age*.

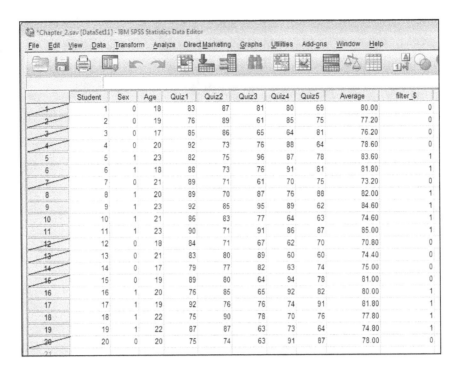

Figure 14-4. *Diagonal lines indicate filtered records*

Descriptive Statistics

	N	Minimum	Maximum	Mean	Std. Deviation
Student Age	10	18	23	21.10	1.792
Valid N (listwise)	10				

Figure 14-5. *Descriptive Statistics indicate that only females are included*

Sorting Records

You can sort the data file on one or more variables to make the data set more orderly. If you need to split a file, you must sort it. SPSS can perform the sort procedure independently of the file split or at the same time. For illustrative purposes, we will perform the sort procedure separately from the file split.

To perform the sorting operation, first make sure all cases are selected. Click on **Data > Select Cases> All Cases**. Now click on **Data > Sort Cases** (see Figure 14-6).

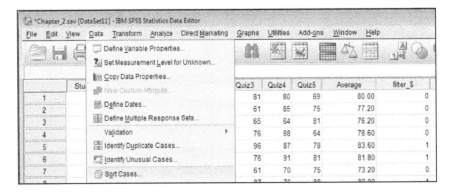

Figure 14-6. *Click Data > Sort Cases*

In the resulting dialog, you can enter one or more variables on which to sort. We will enter *Sex* and then *Age*. Accept the default to sort the records in ascending order (see Figure 14-7).

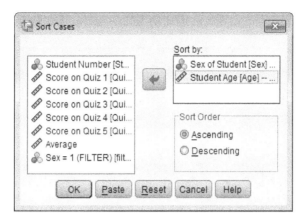

Figure 14-7. Sort Cases dialog

When you click **OK**, the records will be sorted by *Age* within *Sex*, as examination of the Data View verifies (see Figure 14-8). As you have learned already, having a record number makes it easy to return the data set to the original order if you choose to do so by sorting on that number.

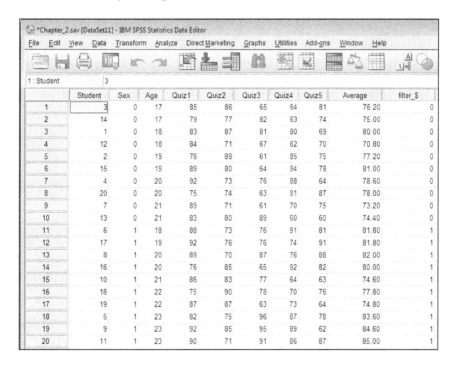

Figure 14-8. Cases sorted by Age within Sex

Splitting a File

Splitting a file creates separate layers, and works in a fashion similar to selecting cases—with one exception. When you split the file, any analyses you perform will be conducted for each group (or "layer"). This is a very convenient and efficient way to avoid conducting the same procedure repetitively. As indicated above, you have to sort the records in order to split the file, but if the records are not already sorted, the Split File menu gives you the option of sorting them.

We will split the file by *Sex*. Select **Data** > **Split File** (see Figure 14-9). A dialog will appear. Move *Sex* to the "Groups Based on" field. You can choose to have SPSS compare the results by group or to perform separate analyses for each group. In our case, we will elect to organize the output to compare groups. Because we have previously sorted the file, click on the radio button next to "File is already sorted" (see Figure 4-10).

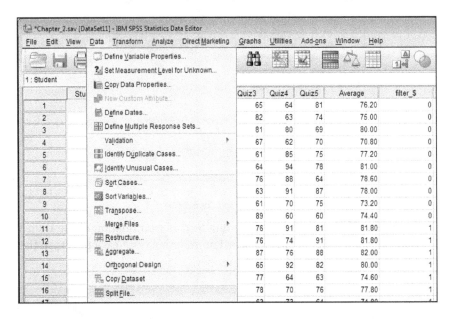

Figure 14-9. *Select Data > Split File*

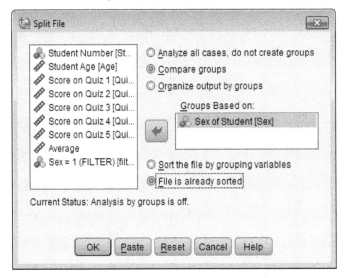

Figure 14-10. *Split File dialog*

When you click on **OK**, the file will be split until you turn off the split by selecting "Analyze all cases, do not create groups" (see Figure 14-10).

We will verify the split by calculating descriptive statistics for *Age*. Select **Analyze** > **Descriptive Statistics** > **Descriptives**, and move *Age* to the Variables field (see Figure 14-11).

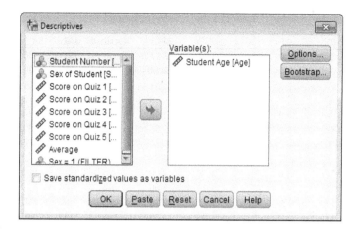

Figure 14-11. Descriptives dialog

Now click on **OK** to run the procedure. The SPSS Viewer output now has separated the descriptive statistics for *Male* and *Female* (see Figure 14-12).

Descriptive Statistics

Sex of Student		N	Minimum	Maximum	Mean	Std. Deviation
Male	Student Age	10	17	21	19.00	1.491
	Valid N (listwise)	10				
Female	Student Age	10	18	23	21.10	1.792
	Valid N (listwise)	10				

Figure 14-12. Split file produces output for each group

Recoding a Variable

Recoding is helpful in such situations as establishing grouping levels, dealing with outliers or missing data, coding string variables to numbers, or reverse-scoring a scale item. You recode variables by assigning new values to old values. These new values can replace the original variable or can be recoded into a different variable.

The following data are from 22 college freshmen (See table 14-1 and data file Chapter_14.sav). Variables include the number of hours taken as a freshman, the student's sex, high school grade point average (on a 5-point scale), college grade point average (on a 4-point scale), whether the student returned as a sophomore and the student's scores on the SAT-Verbal and SAT-Math subscales.

Table 14-1. *Freshman retention data*

ID	FreshHrs	Sex	HSGPA	CollGPA	Retained	SATV	SATM
1	18.0	M	3.96	2.17	No	600	450
2	13.0	F	3.10	2.14	No	470	420
3	16.0	F	4.79	3.81	No	510	590
4	16.0	F	4.85	3.38	No	590	670
5	13.0	F	3.29	2.08	No	380	420
6	15.0	F	2.22	1.56	No	480	430
7	16.0	F	4.28	3.81	No	590	570
8	16.0	F	2.79	2.88	No	440	470
9	15.0	F	3.78	2.00	No	530	590
10	14.0	F	3.03	3.00	No	580	470
11	17.0	M	2.72	2.38	Yes	480	380
12	15.0	F	3.86	3.33	Yes	490	540
13	13.0	F	3.30	1.62	Yes	490	510
14	15.0	F	3.17	1.80	Yes	390	450
15	13.0	M	3.80	3.00	Yes	450	450
16	16.0	F	4.21	3.31	Yes	530	660
17	16.0	F	4.48	2.81	Yes	570	430
18	17.0	M	4.38	3.47	Yes	600	670
19	16.0	F	4.40	3.19	Yes	540	530
20	17.0	M	3.30	2.59	Yes	390	610
21	16.0	F	3.80	3.81	Yes	480	610
22	15.0	F	4.21	2.87	Yes	480	520

Before performing any analyses, you would like to recode the student's sex as 1 (*Male*) and 2 (*Female*) and retention as 0 (*No*) and 1 (*Yes*). You might also like to create a total score for the SAT by adding the two subscales for each student. As you recall from Chapter 2, you can use the **Transform** > **Compute Variable** menu to compute and save a new variable. The Transform menu is also used to recode the old values into new values for *Sex* and *Retention*.

Enter the data in SPSS (see Figure 14-13) or retrieve the file from the companion web page. Establish a data structure and label the variables and values appropriately.

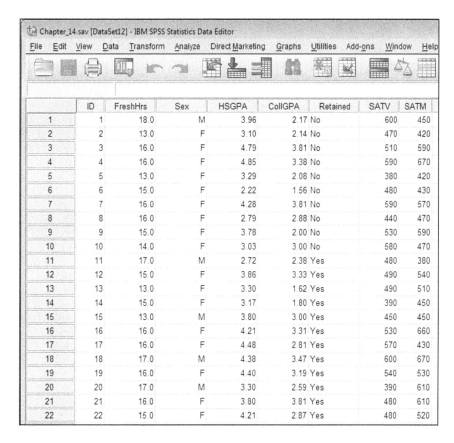

Figure 14-13. Freshman retention data

Sex and *Retained* are string variables. We want to recode them as numbers and change the type to numeric. To recode *Sex*, select **Transform** > **Recode into Same Variables** (see Figure 14-14).

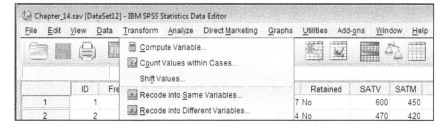

Figure 14-14. Select Transform > Recode into Same Variables

In the dialog, move *Sex* into the Variables window and then click on **Old and New Values** (see Figure 14-15).

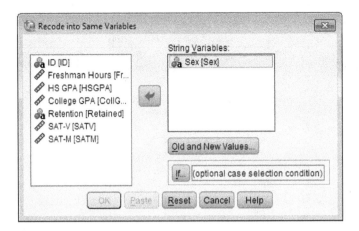

Figure 14-15. Recode into Same Variables dialog

Enter *M* as the old value and 1 as the new value for males, and then click on **Add**. Now enter *F* as the old value and 2 as the new value for females, and then click on **Add**. See Figure 14-16. SPSS supplies the quote marks for string entries.

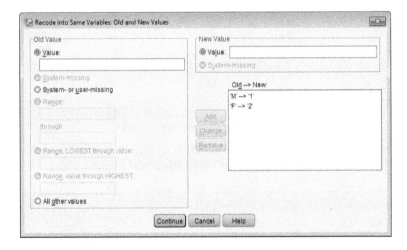

Figure 14-16. Old and New Values dialog

Click **Continue**. You can change the data type for *Sex* to numeric (nominal) in the Variable view. Repeat the recoding process with *Retained* to change *No* to 0 and *Yes* to 1 (see Figure 14-17).

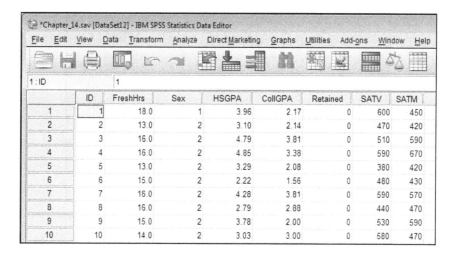

Figure 14-17. Sex and Retention are recoded

Restructuring Data

In Chapter 9 you learned that the repeated-measures ANOVA procedure uses "wide" data, but that to do the equivalent analysis in SPSS Base version, you need to restructure the data into "long" form. A wizard makes this very easy. We will return to the data set from Chapter 9 to illustrate (see Figure 14-18). Note that restructuring the data will modify the data set, and cannot be undone, so you will want to make a backup copy of your original data before restructuring a data file.

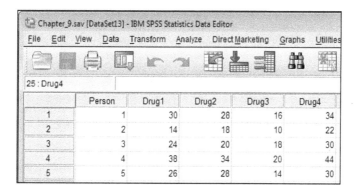

Figure 14-18. Data from Chapter 9

To produce the "long" form, use the **Data** > **Restructure** menu (see Figure 14-19).

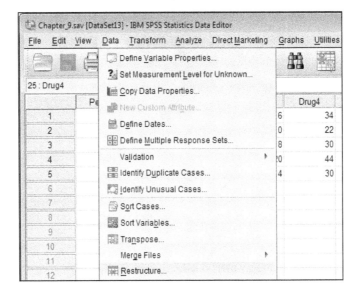

Figure 14-19. *Select Data > Restructure*

In the resulting dialog, select "Restructure selected variables into cases" (see Figure 14-20), and then click **Next**.

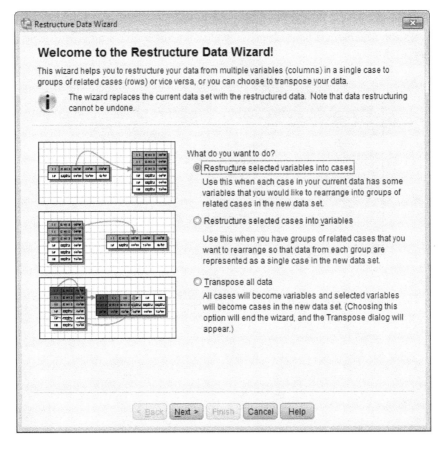

Figure 14-20. *Select Restructure selected variables into cases*

Specify that you want to create one variable group (see Figure 14-21). Click **Next**.

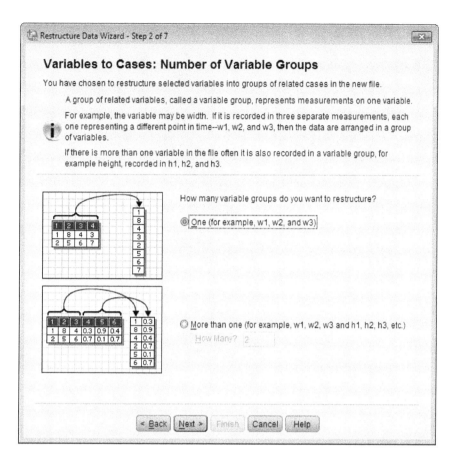

Figure 14-21. Specify one variable group

In the next step, click on "Use selected variable" in the Group Identification field. Move *Person* to that window. Name your target variable *Score*, and then move *Drug1*, *Drug2*, *Drug3*, and *Drug4* to that window (see Figure 14-22). If you have not recorded a participant or case number, SPSS can use the original row number as the group identifier field.

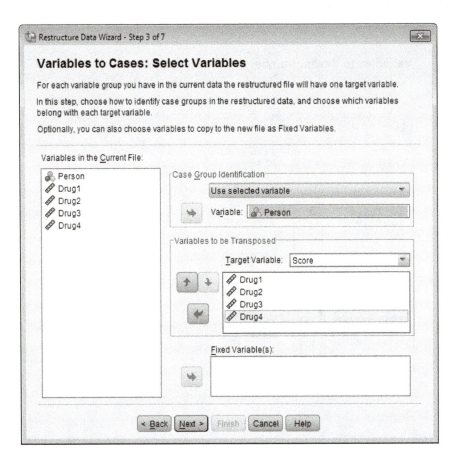

Figure 14-22. Select group identification variable and variables to be transposed

Next, allow SPSS to create an index variable, which will be coded 1, 2, 3, and 4 for the specific drugs (see Figure 14-23).

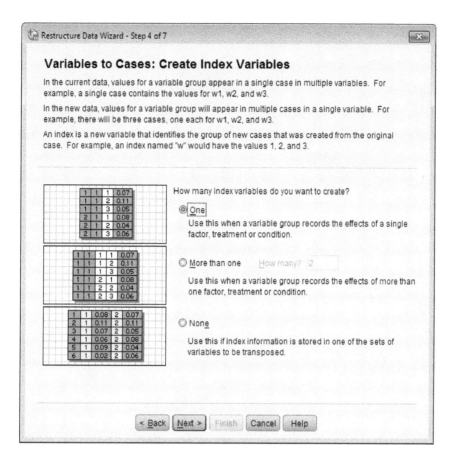

Figure 14-23. *Create one index variable*

In Step 5 (not shown), accept the default to use sequential index values. Click **Next** and accept the defaults in Step 6 (not shown). Click **Next**. Finally, click on **Finish** (see Figure 14-24) to restructure the data into the desired long form (Figure 14-25).

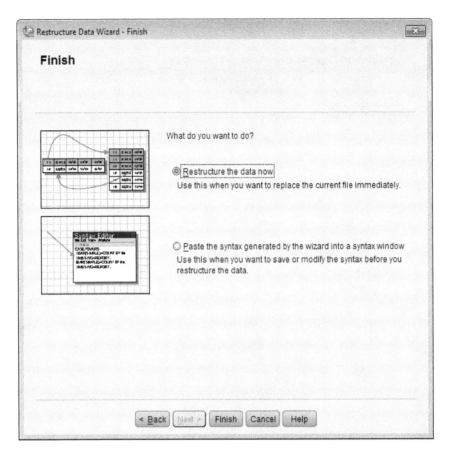

Figure 14-24. Click on Finish to complete the data restructuring

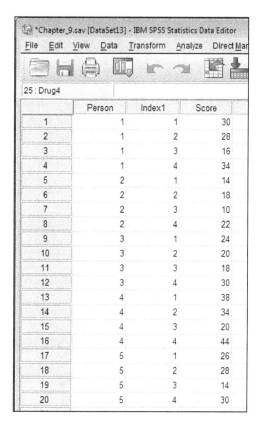

Figure 14-25. Restructured data set

15 Bootstrapping

Objectives

1. Understand bootstrapping.
2. Understand the problems with null hypothesis significance testing.
3. Illustrate bootstrapping with examples.

Overview

As you have examined the SPSS dialog boxes shown in this book, you may have noticed the button labeled "Bootstrap" (for example, look at Figure 14-11, which is reproduced below as Figure 15-1).

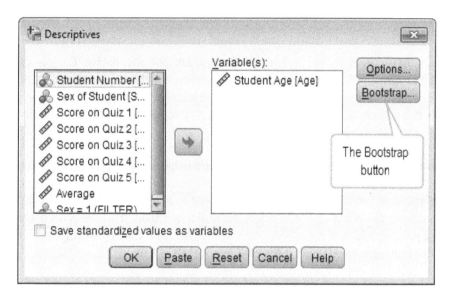

Figure 15-1. See the "Bootstrap" button above

The bootstrap and related techniques are used to deal with data that do not follow parametric assumptions such as linearity, homoscedasticity, or normality of distribution. We also find these techniques useful when we have small samples. These techniques allow us to study the sampling distributions for unusual statistics or even for new ones we come up with on our own. For example, using bootstrapping allows us to develop confidence intervals for the median, and there is no parametric method for that purpose.

A *bootstrap* is a sample with replacement from the same data we began with. It is common to produce around 1000 bootstrap samples, and that is the default in SPSS, though you can change it. It is also customary to use a 95% confidence interval, and that too is the SPSS default.

Some critics object that bootstrapping is "pulling numbers out of thin air" by using the same data values more than once, but remember we use the data to calculate the mean and then use the mean and the original data to calculate the variance and standard deviation. What makes bootstrapping different from traditional statistics is that we are making few or no assumptions about the population, and are in essence generating a sampling distribution of the desired statistic using the numbers in our original data.

The bootstrapping module is an add-on for SPSS, and your version may not have it. You may be interested to know that an alternative is the statistical programming language R, which is an open-source implementation of the language S developed at AT&T. R provides the ability to perform bootstrapping and many other procedures for which SPSS add-on modules are necessary. You can read more about how to do bootstrapping and related techniques in my book *Beginning R: An Introduction to Statistical Programming* (Pace, 2012).

Bootstrapping is only one of the "new" methods of statistics. Techniques like bootstrapping, jackknifing, resampling, and permutation tests have actually been around for many years, but the lack of computing power made their use difficult. Although we will not cover these other techniques here, we will illustrate bootstrapping with a few (interesting, I hope) examples. First, let us examine some of the problems with hypothesis testing.

The Problems and Pitfalls of Hypothesis Testing

In this book, up to this point, you have calculated and displayed descriptive statistics and conducted and interpreted hypothesis tests. There is a growing consensus among modern statisticians that null hypothesis significance testing (NHST) is an anachronism. NHST is based on the work of R. A. Fisher, an eminent statistician of the 20th century. Fisher preferred to talk about p values rather than confidence intervals, and his interpretation of the null hypothesis and the alternative hypothesis have become entrenched, especially among behavioral and social scientists.

We concern ourselves with two competing hypotheses, the null and the alternative. Each is a statement about population parameters or about functions of population parameters such as the difference between means. The null hypothesis is a statement of no effect, no difference, no change, or no relationship in the population. The alternative hypothesis is a statement that there is an effect, a difference, a change, or a relationship in the population.

The null and alternative hypotheses are mutually exclusive and exhaustive. That is, only one can be true and one of them must be true. The problem is that we are talking about *population parameters*, not *sample statistics*. We rarely know the population, and we therefore use sample statistics as estimates of the population parameters. We make a decision as to whether to reject or not to reject the null hypothesis. This decision is based on our sample results. We calculate a p value, which is really a conditional probability, the probability of getting the sample results we obtained, or results more extreme, if the null hypothesis is true.

When we do hypothesis testing using parametric procedures such as t tests and ANOVAs, we must assume certain things about the population. You have learned in this book how to test distributional assumptions by using graphs and hypothesis tests. The most common assumptions are that the data are normally distributed, that the variances are equal in the population, and that data are linear. Another problem is that real life data are not so orderly, and are rarely normally distributed. With large samples, we can invoke the central limit theorem and assume with confidence that the sampling distribution of means will be very close to a normal distribution, but we have no such assurance with small samples.

The problems with the NHST approach to hypothesis testing are therefore manifold. We never prove anything, but simply speak as though we have found support for the alternative hypothesis if we have rejected the null hypothesis. Many critics of NHST point out that this does little to advance knowledge. Because we rarely know the population, we also do not know whether we have committed an error when we make our decision concerning the null hypothesis. In addition, because real data are very disorderly, we often have a mess on our hands when we try to use parametric procedures with such ill-behaved numbers.

Modern Robust Statistics

A class of modern robust statistics has emerged over the last 60 years or so (Erceg-Hurn & Mirosevich, 2008). Somewhat ironically, the very person who gave us NHST also provided the first real alternative, the Fisher Exact Test. The Fisher Exact test is a kind of permutation test. As an alternative to chi-square tests of independence, the Fisher Exact Test provides us with the probability of the current combination of categorical variables in a two-by-two contingency table, and every other combination that is more extreme than the observed one.

We can categorize the modern robust statistics as including:

1. The use of Winsorization, trimmed means, and other techniques to deal with outliers.

2. The use of bootstrapping to resample a data set in order to determine the sampling distribution of a statistic of interest. We typically generate around 1000 samples, as discussed above, and study the distribution as well as develop confidence intervals.

3. The use of permutation tests and related techniques to replace traditional hypothesis testing.

4. The use of modern rank statistics such as the rank transform, ANOVA-type statistics, and other rank-based methods.

Because these techniques do not make assumptions about populations, this whole class of techniques is essentially nonparametric. In addition to developing a simulation in which we generate samples from a normal distribution, we will return to a couple of previous examples and perform bootstrapping analyses, and compare our results to those of the traditional hypothesis tests.

Bootstrapping Confidence Intervals for the Mean

I mentioned SPSS syntax in the preface of this book. I certainly do not intend to teach you how to program in SPSS syntax, but you will see its use here. You should know that if you are using the student version of SPSS, you will not be able to use syntax. Similarly, unless you have access to the Bootstrapping add-on, you will not be able to perform bootstrapping.

We will use SPSS syntax to generate 1000 samples from a normal distribution with a mean of 500 and a standard deviation of 100. Here is the SPSS Syntax Editor window, showing the syntax to generate our variable, which I called x (Figure 15-2).

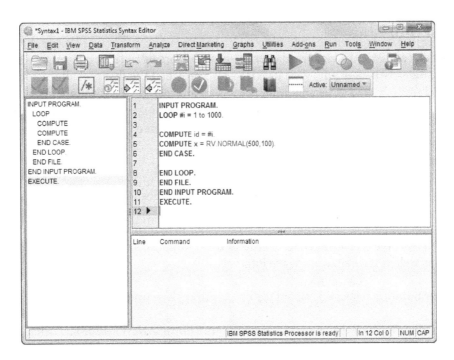

Figure 15-2.*SPSS syntax to produce 1000 samples from a normal distribution with a mean of 500 and standard deviation of 100*

To execute the syntax, you can select all or part of the syntax and click on the big green right-pointing arrow in the icon bar, or alternatively, you can select **Run > All** (Figure 15-3).

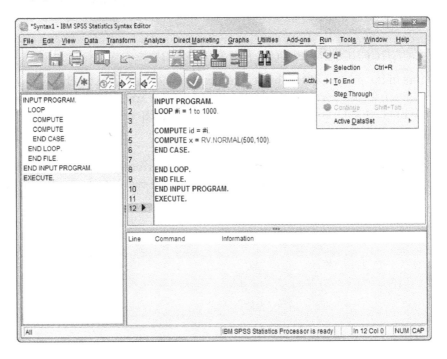

Figure 15-3. *Select Run > All to execute the syntax*

Here are the first several lines of our new data file (Figure 15-4). Note that the ID number is technically not necessary, but as we discussed previously, having it allows us more easily to identify individual records when we sort and filter the data.

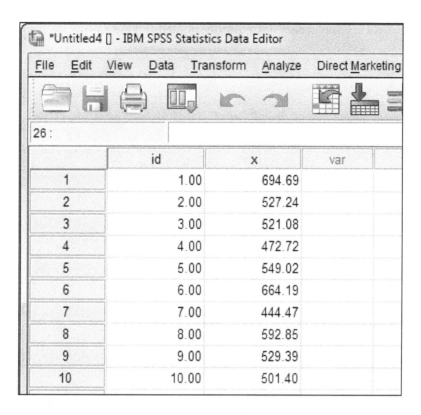

Figure 15-4. The first 10 records of our new data file

First, let us calculate the mean and standard deviation of our new random data and find a 95% confidence interval for the mean. Select **Analyze** > **Descriptive Statistics** > **Explore**. Select the options to display a histogram, and select a 95% confidence interval. Here is our descriptive statistics summary (Figure 15-5). Unsurprisingly, the mean of our 1000 samples is very close to 500, and the standard deviation is very close to 100.

Descriptives

			Statistic	Std. Error
x	Mean		504.7948	3.16745
	95% Confidence Interval for Mean	Lower Bound	498.5792	
		Upper Bound	511.0105	
	5% Trimmed Mean		504.8702	
	Median		506.1118	
	Variance		10032.765	
	Std. Deviation		100.16369	
	Minimum		220.69	
	Maximum		822.79	
	Range		602.09	
	Interquartile Range		137.88	
	Skewness		-.001	.077
	Kurtosis		-.151	.155

Figure 15-5. Descriptive statistics for our 1000 samples.

The histogram shows the data are very nearly normally distributed (Figure 15-6).

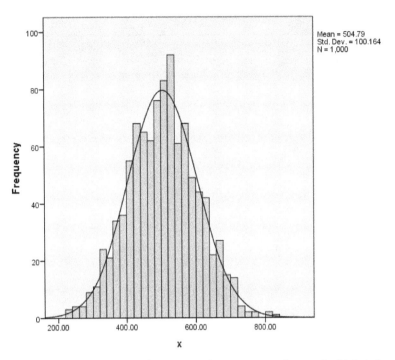

Figure 15-6. Histogram shows our sample means are nearly normally distributed

Now, let us generate 1000 bootstrap samples from our data and calculate the mean and confidence interval for those samples. To do this, select **Analyze > Descriptive Statistics > Descriptives**. Enter x as the variable (Figure 15-7), and choose the mean as the only desired statistic.

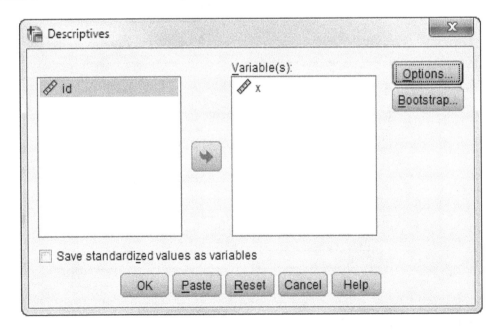

Figure 15-7. Preparing to bootstrap the mean and confidence interval

Next, click on **Bootstrap** (see Figure 15-8). Accept all the defaults.

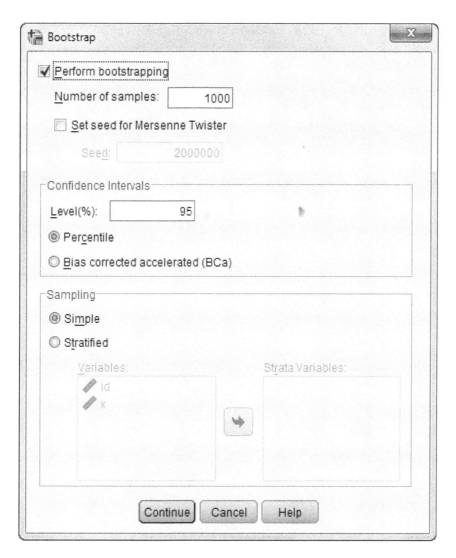

Figure 15-8. *Accept all the defaults*

When you click on **Continue**, SPSS generates the 1000 samples and then provides a summary (See Figure 15-9).

Descriptive Statistics

			Bootstrap[a]			
					95% Confidence Interval	
		Statistic	Bias	Std. Error	Lower	Upper
x	N	1000	0	0	1000	1000
	Mean	504.7948	-.0830	3.1464	498.4826	510.6879
Valid N (listwise)	N	1000	0	0	1000	1000

a. Unless otherwise noted, bootstrap results are based on 1000 bootstrap samples

Figure 15-9. *Results of our bootstrapping experiment*

Obviously, our mean and confidence limits will be similar, but not identical to those found from the original data.

You may be wondering that if bootstrapping and parametric methods produce the same or similar results, why bother to do bootstrapping? The answer is that the two methods do not always produce the same results, and that modern robust statistical methods will eventually replace or at least supersede NHST, so there is no better time to learn these "new" techniques than the present. Another answer is that you can do things with bootstrapping that are impossible or difficult to do with parametric procedures. For our next example, we will bootstrap the median rather than the mean. We continue with our *x* variable.

Bootstrapping the Median

For this demonstration, select **Analyze > Descriptive Statistics > Frequencies**. Choose the median as the only statistic of interest (Figure 15-10).

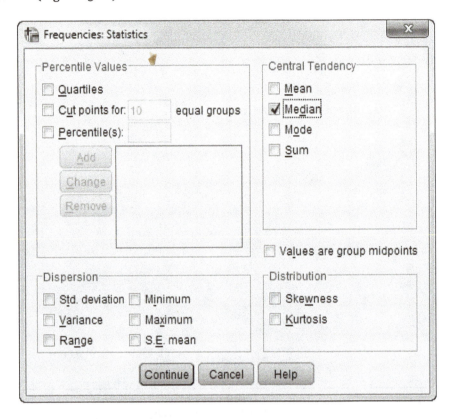

Figure 15-10. Select the median as the statistic of interest.

Click **Continue**, and then select the *x* variable and click **Bootstrap**. As before, accept all defaults, and the click **Continue** and **OK** to run the analysis. As the screens are repetitive, they are not shown. Instead, examine the results of our bootstrapping of the median (Figure 15-11). Because the distribution is nearly normal, the median is very close to the mean, and has very similar confidence limits.

Statistics

x

			Bootstrap[a]			
					95% Confidence Interval	
		Statistic	Bias	Std. Error	Lower	Upper
N	Valid	1000	0	0	1000	1000
	Missing	0	0	0	0	0
Median		506.1118	-.4498	3.3858	499.0846	512.4685

a. Unless otherwise noted, bootstrap results are based on 1000 bootstrap samples

Figure 15-11. Bootstrapping the median of our data set

Bootstrapping the Difference Between Means

As our final demonstration, let us return to the data from Chapter 6, in which we performed an independent-samples *t* test. Recall that we compared the mean body temperatures for males and females. For convenience, the output appears below (see Figure 15-12).

Group Statistics

	Participant Sex	N	Mean	Std. Deviation	Std. Error Mean
Body Temperature	Male	64	98.133	.6660	.0832
	Female	63	98.387	.6427	.0810

Independent Samples Test

		Levene's Test for Equality of Variances		t-test for Equality of Means						
									95% Confidence Interval of the Difference	
		F	Sig.	t	df	Sig. (2-tailed)	Mean Difference	Std. Error Difference	Lower	Upper
Body Temperature	Equal variances assumed	.575	.450	-2.191	125	.030	-.2545	.1162	-.4844	-.0246
	Equal variances not assumed			-2.191	124.95	.030	-.2545	.1161	-.4843	-.0247

Figure 15-12. Independent-samples t-test results

To do the bootstrapping, click on **Bootstrap** from the independent-samples *t* test dialog (Figure 15-13).

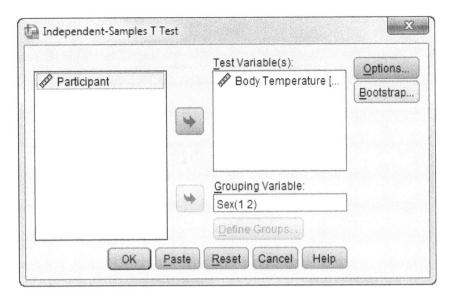

Figure 15-13. Click on Bootstrap to perform the analysis.

Accept all the defaults and observe the final output (Figure 15-14).

Independent Samples Test

		Levene's Test for Equality of Variances		t-test for Equality of Means						
									95% Confidence Interval of the Difference	
		F	Sig.	t	df	Sig. (2-tailed)	Mean Difference	Std. Error Difference	Lower	Upper
Body Temperature	Equal variances assumed	.575	.450	-2.191	125	.030	-.2545	.1162	-.4844	-.0246
	Equal variances not assumed			-2.191	124.952	.030	-.2545	.1161	-.4843	-.0247

Bootstrap for Independent Samples Test

			Bootstrap[a]				
		Mean Difference	Bias	Std. Error	Sig. (2-tailed)	95% Confidence Interval	
						Lower	Upper
Body Temperature	Equal variances assumed	-.2545	.0048	.1146	.039	-.4820	-.0007
	Equal variances not assumed	-.2545	.0048	.1146	.039	-.4820	-.0007

a. Unless otherwise noted, bootstrap results are based on 1000 bootstrap samples

Figure 15-14. Results of bootstrapping the mean difference

We now can compare the results of the parametric procedure (independent samples *t* test) with those of the bootstrap procedure. We see that as with the confidence intervals for the mean, the mean differences, the *p* values, and the confidence intervals for the mean differences are very similar with both the parametric test and the bootstrapping approach. We are benefitting here from the central limit theorem and the fact that we have a relatively large sample size. When the sample sizes are smaller, and when the data are not so orderly, the two techniques can often produce very different results. When that is the case, the modern robust approach is more likely to be closer to the truth than the traditional parametric approach.

References

Cronk, B. (2008). *How to use SPSS: A step-by-step guide to analysis and interpretation* (5th ed.). Glendale, CA: Pyrczak Publishing.

Ecreg-Hurn, D. M., & Mirosevich, V. M. (2008). Modern robust statistical methods: An easy way to maximize the accuracy and power of your research. *American Psychologist, 63*, 591-601.

Field, A. (2005). *Discovering statistics using SPSS* (2nd ed.). London: Sage Publications.

George, D., & Mallery, P. (2009). *SPSS for Windows step-by-step: A simple guide and reference 16.0 update* (9th ed.). New York: Allyn & Bacon.

Green, S., Salkind, N. (2009*). Using SPSS for Windows and Macintosh: Analyzing and understanding data* (5th ed.). Upper Saddle River, NJ: Prentice Hall.

Norušis, M. (2009). *SPSS 16.0 guide to data analysis*. Upper Saddle River, NJ: Prentice Hall.

Pace, L. (2008). *Point-and-click! Guide to SPSS for Windows* (4th ed.). Anderson, SC: TwoPaces, LLC.

Pace, L. (2008, May). Laptops in the classroom: help or hype? Poster presented at the 2008 Annual Convention of the Association for Psychological Science/ STP Teaching Institute, Chicago.

Pace, L. (2012). *Beginning R: An introduction to statistical programming*. New York, NY: Apress.

Sweet, S., & Grace-Martin, K. (2008). *Data analysis with SPSS: A first course in applied statistics* (3rd ed.). New York: Allyn & Bacon.

Index

www.ingramcontent.com/pod-product-compliance
Lightning Source LLC
Chambersburg PA
CBHW080418060326
40689CB00019B/4288